This is a true story – a biography/autobiography
I found that I was unable to write this story so near to my heart with the names
we had always used and so I changed them and wrote the memories in third
person. All else is factual including the location of Fayetteville, Texas.

This book was printed by CreateSpace, an Amazon.com Company
Available from Amazon.com, CreateSpace.com, and other retail outlets.

ISBN;   10:0615882544
ISBN – 13;978-0615882543;

Only the Laughter

Barbara McAllister

Dedication

My family comes first in all things.
I dedicate this work to my daughters
Dianne, Mae Claire, Sophia and their children.
I also dedicate this to my husband Mac
And all of those whom I love or have ever loved.

CONTENTS

This book was printed by CreateSpace, An Amazon.com Company

Available from Amazon.com, CreateSpace.com, and other retail outlets.

Introduction

Light Years

Jim wanted to write the body of this work and his title would have been *Light Years* but the pace of things became too fast for him. Time went by quickly as the disease that was taking his life progressed and he was unable to complete his task. So, as a gift of love to him and my Rachel, I will try to tell their story.

I have chosen the title *Only the Laughter* because I prefer to remember the laughter we all shared during those short years with Jim and those Rachel continued on without him.

All was not easy as you will see but don't think that this is only a sad tale of lives cut short. This is a love story, a record of the beauty and struggles of life and the value of time.

Acknowledgements

First recognition must go to Jim for his hard work under extremely difficult circumstances as he tried to record his journey through ALS using the beam on his light talker to operate his computer. He was unable to complete his book which was to be called *Light Years* but the sections that my daughter saved of it are included here. Her words are here also and I could not have completed the story without their participation so long ago. The boy I call Sean, wrote the poem, *San Antone?* Jim's poem *The Elusive Dream*, and the combined efforts of Jim and the daughter I call Rachel produced the poem *T'wer the Night before Christmas.* Jim's mother's letter was in the file with his work on Light Years. Jim's family is and was extraordinary, his sister – a teacher like her mother, his brother an attorney and both dedicated to Jim. His mother died within a few weeks of Rachel. She was a fine lady with great courage. His family never failed Jim and Rachel and were there giving and loving as you will see when you read *Only the Laughter.* My husband Mac designed the cover which is a photograph of the farm house we lived in in Fayette County. Texas, taken while we lived there. This book would never have been written and published without the love and help of all of my family.

Remembering

Sometimes, when death comes, sorrow overshadows the joy of the life that was and so when the Anderson family first knew that Jim Mitchell was coming into their lives, they decided they would not allow his approaching death to replace the good. They would make the best of the short time they were to have with him. They would do this for Jim, but little did they know just how much he would influence all of their lives and prepare them for things to come. They would collect the laughter they shared, that precious element necessary to sustain the human spirit, and carry it with them on their own life's journey.

Chapter One
Sentimental Moments

Kate Anderson sat at her computer deep in thought listening to the theme song from *Somewhere in Time* - a tape Jim had given her. In her mind, she was not here in this room. She was once again on the farm in Fayette County during the days when she had her Rachel and that daughter's little flock of boys beneath her wings. She could see herself there in that farmhouse working at her keyboard. Her hair was not silver as it was today, but as it had been back then, black and frizzed in its usual way due to the moist air and perspiration on her brow.

On that long ago afternoon she had been working on her first novel, that mythical quest long scoffed at by family and friends. Now that book was in print and Rachel had been the main catalyst to make that happen.

A Miller bug struggled against the windowpane above her desk. As if she could no longer bear his mindless search for freedom, Kate grasped the window, raised it, and gently guided the frantic creature toward the opening.

Sometimes it is the little things that make us smile and she smiled now as she watched the tiny insect fluttering happily on his way. Its flight made her think of Jim, bound to that wheelchair and never wanting to see anything caged or held against its will.

....

The upfront facts were that Jim Mitchell was a man of 32 young years who had been diagnosed at the age of 30 with ALS. Rachel Anderson became his nurse near the beginning of his illness. During those days the most memorable words said about him at the Anderson house was that he was a bit of a monster to care for.

A more significant fact learned at a later date was that Jim could be a rogue and had been known most of his young years as a lady's man. He could charm a leaf off of a tree and what he could do to the ladies was whatever he chose for the most part. His silver tongue was well known and his nurses all immediately fell in love with him to one degree or another, with the exception of Rachel. In her, he found his match and she took little of his sarcastic lip. In his anger at his illness, he took aim at this particular nurse. Maybe that was true because he loved nothing better than a good argument and she gave that to him. During their first year, she usually headed for home after each shift extremely grateful that that was over and she could briefly forget about her patient and the stress of being near him.

Jim was married to a woman older than himself who had a 16 year old daughter but he had no children of his own. He had been somewhat happy during his years with this wife, until he became ill. At this place in time, Jim was still ambulatory but could not use his hands and his speech was slurred and difficult to understand. The disease was progressing quickly, and his marriage was failing.

After approximately a year of being Jim's nurse, Rachel's family decided to move out of Houston and she was going with them to Fayette County, Texas where they were to begin their new lease on life. She would commute in order to keep her job with the Houston nursing service and remain Jim's nurse. It was **late summer of 1988.**

....

Rachel's parents were country people and city life was foreign to them in every way. They had lived all over the state of Texas during their years together but Houston had become the most hectic and stressful. Added to the smothering effect of life in that bubbling mass of humanity was Keith's poor health, high school and college expenses, IRS audits, daughters' divorces and what Kate referred to as boy trouble. For her, last, but up near the top of the list, had to be the chore of driving to work every day in Houston traffic.

Now, Keith was off of dialysis with his new kidney and didn't have to live so near his doctors or a dialysis center. It was time for the family to go back to the country. The Andersons read every small town newspaper they could find for a year. Finally the LaGrange paper had an ad seeking renters for a country house and acreage near Fayetteville. It sounded promising and so the appointment was made. Today they were meeting with the owners of the property.

Kate loved Fayetteville on sight but tried to remain neutral about all of it until she could see the farm. The tiny hamlet is and was when the Anderson's first saw it, a beautiful historic living replica of a Texas town from long ago, a treasure, serene and simple.

Fayetteville, Texas was once a thriving community in a place off the beaten path. The Andersons had passed by the Fayetteville turnoff over a period of thirty years traveling from Houston to Austin and never noted its existence even though a large sign invited visitors to come. They turned east off of Hwy 71 and followed a narrow paved road. The pleasant drive ended with the view of a cluster of small houses spattered here and there, a water tower to their right and children running beside the road. The first business they saw was a tiny gas station with a variety of odd items stuffed in the windows and two overweight gentlemen visiting in the driveway.

They drove around for a short tour of the town which had many empty, long deserted houses waiting for a family to return and bring them life again. The occupied homes had toys in the well-kept yards. A precinct courthouse sat in the center of the town square. There was a schoolhouse which they soon learned was originally established by the Catholic Church, a bank, post office, general mercantile store, dry goods store, Justice of the Peace office, hardware store with a funeral parlor in the back, two barber shops, three cafés, a museum, a butane service, three service stations, an auto repair shop and laundry and a variable number of antique stores. Two blocks east of the square a Catholic church boasted the largest membership of the local churches and a small Lutheran congregation on the west side of town tried to keep up. A Church of Christ fellowship marked its presence on a small house beside the defunct movie theatre which was attached to the building that had once housed the Red and White grocery store.

The three restaurants were quite a number for a town of such a small population but all were busy. The prospective landlord had set their meeting at Orsak's Café located on the town square. It was what many would call a hole in the wall sort of place. Like the rest of the structures in this little town, the building apparently had been there for a very long time.

When Kate entered the front door, it rattled behind her and the floor creaked beneath her feet. Other than that, there was dead silence. A dining counter was to the right and the obvious proprietor of the place stood behind it. He was tall with a shock of white hair and a quick smile. He was apparently also the cook since he was wearing a dirty apron, which he was using as a hand towel at the moment. All tables were occupied as well as the seats at the counter. Kate looked about the room filled with eyes centered on her and her spouse. Who were these strangers?

No one seemed dressed to go out. The men had on their work hats with sweat rings around the crown and some of the women had wrapped their heads in scarves to cover whatever their hair looked like. Toward the back of the room they saw two people who seemed out of place. They must be the landlord and spouse.

The male part of the equation was a tall slender man, who possessed a somewhat blank face and the look of a Berkley University professor. He and his wife were dressed casually. He was wearing Khaki and she wore bobby socks and a dress. Kate thought they had the appearance of someone from back east and not Texas. The female of the pair was obviously a person with the attitude of someone from the late 60s, a flower child at heart. Her gray hair was parted slightly off center and a few strands of it hung limply beside her face. Kate couldn't decide if she had been attractive in her youth or not.

All introduced themselves and sat down to have breakfast and a question and answer session. A trip to the prospective farm followed. All during their time in Orsak's café, Kate was certain there were lip readers in the room who would make a full report to the rest of the crowd as soon as they left.

When they first saw the farm, the hills surrounding it left only the second floor of the house visible from the road. The cattle guard was narrow and the ditches beside it were overgrown with tall weeds. A small, early Texas farmhouse sat to the right just inside the gate. It had broken windows and the look of something that had been dropped from a truck and left at an uncomfortable tilt. Hopefully, this was not the place that was for rent. Kate was relieved to find that it was not. As the suburban crossed through the gate they could see an overgrown one way road headed due west from there, slowly curving up hill to the south. Several large ponds rested just below the curve. Beside one of the ponds, another old farm cottage had been dumped, though shaken up by that event, it stood on unsteady blocks, trying to keep from sliding into the nearby pond. It had a small porch on the front and stairs going up the outside wall. The tiny house (later to be tagged the fishing shack) leaned forward slightly, as if searching for fish in the pond.

The road climbed and then another gate with a cattle guard left them in an open area facing a once white picket fence with many boards hanging loose or on the ground. A trellis stood at the gate waiting to welcome them. Beyond the fence was a large yellow farm house with a porch facing the gate and Kate could see another (screened) porch toward the back on the other side. There were two cottages in the yard. One (painted red) appeared to be a smokehouse. A yellow building to the right of the side gate was apparently the well house. Various sheds were scattered here and there and a huge barn with stock pens beyond stood a few yards from the cattle guard. A large mound of dirt partially blocked their view of the larger of the cottages. The grass inside the gate had been recently mowed but weeds were everywhere and the place looked as if it had been abandoned for some time. Several large trees shaded the yard.

On the east side of the clutter of buildings was a concrete tennis court. It stood complete with a nice net and backdrops. North of the tennis court was a chicken house with doors open and window flaps braced upward.

They were surprised when two old dogs came out to meet them. They soon found that one of the dogs was almost blind and the other stone deaf. They were sweet friendly little souls and Kate liked them right away. The feelings seemed mutual. The landlord explained that the dogs came with the house and were "better off here than in Austin, besides, they always had food and water." When they reached the front door, which was the entrance to the kitchen, Keith pointed to a large feeder running over with dog food which was working alive with fire ants. It was obvious that the dogs had had to find their sustenance elsewhere.

A number of things belonging to the landlord's family remained in the house and it was explained that some would be removed, such as rifles, clothing, furniture, dishes, books, and things of that sort, but others would stay if the Anderson's didn't mind.

The house was unlocked.

Keith was dismayed and discouraged but Kate loved the place on sight. She could see curtains at the windows, floors polished, a little bit of paint here and there and it would be perfect. When her husband saw her face, he knew he had lost the battle already.

A two year lease of the house, including all buildings on the premises, and 52 acres of land was signed and the landlords left the Anderson's to contemplate what they had done.

Whether right or wrong, the dye was cast. The arrangements were shortly made in Houston for both families, Keith and Kate and their daughter Rachel and her boys to move to the country.

Soon they were there, and the adventure began.

Chapter Two

Fayetteville

The Andersons soon discovered that the clocks had stopped decades ago in this very small metropolis. This was evident from the looks of it but the mindset of a few of the local citizens seemed to have ceased to move into modern thinking as well. Prejudices from years past were as Kate remembered those from her own Texas childhood. Certain behaviors were not tolerated and if one pushed too far past the guidelines they just might find a dead chicken hanging over their front door some unexpected morning. Everyone's life was the business of their neighbor and although most of the people were related to one another they seldom admitted even the possibility of such a thing. If a man's name was Snickerman, he would say when asked that he was definitely not any relation to the other Snickerman who lived down the road in this small town of 250+ people - and no one had better say anything different. A usual question asked of newcomers was "Who are your people?" Who you might be related to seemed to be important. The impression given now and then was that the Germans there didn't always like the Czechs and the Czechs didn't care much for them either. Those of a different skin color were not all that welcome and were met with scowls and deeds of indifference.

Some of the old fashioned ideas weren't so bad because the prices from the 1920s were also intact and the local handyman worked cheap, yard work was almost free of charge, and the only drawback was that no one got in a hurry about anything whatsoever. If your carpenter came and worked on your house he finished at his own pace and in his own time which usually resulted in weeks to complete a task that should have taken half a day. The local grocery store which stood on the corner of the square usually had a pile of empty cardboard boxes on the sidewalk out front but a persistent customer could find his way through. The rest of the place had the same feeling as the entrance but everything was accessible. Garrison Keillor's description of Ralph's Pretty Good Grocery Store in Lake Woebegone would fit here. "If Ralph didn't have it, you didn't need it." The store sold items that had no date of expiration because no one knew how many years they had been on the shelf anyway. However, if you were searching for something necessary, they had it there for you. Milk, eggs, and vegetables were plentiful but the staples were sometimes questionable. Medicinal remedies long abandoned by the rest of the modern world were there for the asking and often worked surprisingly well.

The very best, fresh, always tender and delicious meat anyone could want was in abundant supply at Birch's Meat Market, which was next door. It was family owned and operated. They raised their own meat for the most part and Kate was surprised and pleased to be able to buy any and all meats she wanted there on the square in Fayetteville.

All paths seemed to lead to the tiny town square which framed the precinct courthouse. Beside the courthouse, attached like an absent minded idea, the fire station stood with doors open displaying an outdated fire truck that was sufficient for the town fathers, possibly because no one had needed it for some time.

There was little to not like about this country town and in spite of the faults mentioned about local attitudes, most of the people here were kind and gentle, and life was calm, beautiful, and interesting along narrow tree shaded streets.

The towns claim to fame included a tale that the infamous pair, Bonnie Parker and Clyde Barrow, had once stopped in at the Red and White Grocery now out of business with only the name remaining on the sign above the door; and on another occasion a man had been shot to death while being held on the second floor of the precinct courthouse. He happened to be a member of a group with dark pigmented skin and he had done some unforgivable thing or so the locals said. No one was ever arrested for his murder because the man needed shooting and the whole event was cheap justice. Whether either story was true or not no one knew or would say for certain.

The area was mostly populated by the proud descendants of Czechoslovakian immigrants who arrived in Texas among the earliest settlers and believed Fayetteville to be the true cradle of Czech settlement in the state of Texas. Perhaps it was their Czech heritage or the mixture of nationalities here that caused many of the residents to have a somewhat odd way of pronouncing words. For example, if a word began with the letter V it was pronounced with a W sound, which produced a conversation that sounded somewhat Cajun. A veterinarian was a weterinarian. Example: I had to take my cow to the wet today. The Cajun comedian, Justin Wilson could have had long conversations in Orsak's café and completely blended in with the crowd. Their manner of speaking only added more flavor to the spice of life in this unique community.

The Santa Fe railroad line made a sharp turn on the edge of town, its trains slowing for the curve but never stopping, and always disturbing the peace by announcing their passing. The necessity of slowing down because of the curve added entertainment for the kids who still counted the boxcars and placed pennies on the rails when there was nothing else to do. Huge excitement came when the state of Texas considered putting a high speed rail line through Fayetteville. The joke was, they were going to sell tickets for folks to watch it take that curve (at 200 miles per hour) on its way to and from Houston, San

Antonio, and Dallas. Now, that would be something to see.

In ancient days Fayette County had been covered with large trees, a forest perhaps. This was evident from the petrified wood which peppered the fields. There among the petrified wood were arrowheads and other evidence of the Native American tribes who had, eons ago, made their homes here as well.

During recent history, the Czech farmers had grown yams and cotton and whatever they pleased in the fertile ground. They no longer raised these crops but depended on things to feed their cattle. Produce trucks were seldom seen on the highway and the country side was somewhat sleepy, much like the town of Fayetteville. Gravel was plentiful throughout the county and a multitude of gravel trucks bounced along the narrow roads.

Artesian wells had flourished in the area until sometime in the thirties or forties. The rains once plentiful, had dried up somewhat over multiple decades and most wells were no longer spouting fountains of water. However, their remains produced many springs which usually kept the creek beds and ponds full of water, and some of the fish in those ponds were huge.

The summer the Anderson family decided to make their home in Fayetteville brought about changes for them and the townspeople as well. What the Anderson's did not realize was that this was to be for them, a time bringing exceptional memories. It would become a part of their lives almost comparable to those America remembers as the years of involvement in World War II. Kate Anderson surmised that this was because Jim became a catalyst of learning for every member of the family in one way or another. Much like the nation during the big war, their spirits would be tested and prepared for what the future was to bring as they shared the moments of laughter, deep sorrow, tremendous happiness, and extreme courage.

Chapter Three

Facing Incurable Illness

Incurable illness and the destruction it causes for a family was not new to the Andersons. Twelve years before the move to Fayetteville, Keith Anderson had been diagnosed with focal glomilialar sclerosis, actually a name given a category of kidney diseases which cause kidney failure and all have the same result – no known cure. The disease that was taking Jim's life was a bigger monster than the kidney disease. Kate knew that and also, she had already had experience with where all of this was taking the family.

In Keith's case, people sometimes reassured her about the future by telling her that at least Keith could stay alive on dialysis. They knew little of such a life. Kate realized that fact and their kind intent, but deep inside it always angered her to hear those words. Her thinking was, if you were dieing from diarrhea or dieing of cancer, the end result was the same. You had to be the one who had it to know enough to understand.

As the saying goes, a listening ear is much better than pretended wisdom.

. . . .

The trip home from Houston following Keith's diagnosis was muddled in Kate's memory now except for the feelings that washed over her during those long miles home to San Angelo.

Kate was numb emotionally and had been since the moment the doctors told her the prognosis for Keith's illness. It was a cold night and as she drove into a Shell station to fill the tank on the Suburban, she realized how many things she would now have to do for herself. Keith was one of those men who believed the car and everything about it was a husband's job. He would not allow her to fill the gas tank or anything that resembled such duties. Besides, it was dangerous for a woman to be seen standing beside a car with strangers passing on a dark night. Now, he slept in the seat beside her. They were both exhausted from the stay in the Methodist Hospital and most of all, still in shock over the news that would set the tone for the rest of their lives together. The thinking was that Keith's kidneys would shut down completely within two years and he would be placed on dialysis with a strong possibility that he would die within five years.

She cried, her tears stinging her face as she waited in the cold wind. Before returning to the car, she braced herself and thought of this good man and their four dear daughters who waited for them. She would sit down with the girls and explain calmly what was ahead and how they would be alright no matter what came as time passed. "We will have each other to hold on to and we will take care of Daddy, always. We will live it all day to day and not let tomorrow control our daily lives. We are going to laugh and love and treasure every moment" ... and so that is what they had done. Things that had once seemed extremely important no longer mattered and they began to find their happiness in the little moments of life. All past plans for their future were thrown to the wind and had to be forgotten.

When they discovered the disease, Kate was 37 years old and

her young husband 42. They had shared sixteen happy years of marriage but with the assault of the kidney disease, nothing would remain as it had been before. Keith might have continued on with some semblance of fairly normal health if it had not been for the doctors efforts to cure his illness. Huge doses of steroids, affected him immediately. Their damage seemed to hasten his decline and the results became permanent.

Kate hit the books and studied all she could find about the illness. She went to a nutritionist and decided if the doctors couldn't help her husband, she was going to try. They had made some progress and the field of medicine improved as well. Keith had been under treatment for seven years by the summer of 1983; on kidney dialysis for three more, and in 1986, had had a kidney transplant – a gift of life from his brother Kenneth. This transplant gave the family an opportunity to recover some of the lost years and begin again. They had been warned that his disease could and most likely would, take the new kidney but maybe they had some time to live a normal life before that happened. They learned to tell one another "Today we are okay." It was true and somehow gave them respite from the future they knew would come.

Chapter Four

The Andersons

Who the Anderson's were… and the Days ahead……..It would begin with the end of summer heat, a cold winter following, and then a full year of four seasons there on the farm with the family preparing for their future before Jim Mitchell was to become a part of their lives.

Late summer, 1988,

One of the selling points of leasing the farm had been the cottage in the yard (four rooms and a bath) where Rachel and her boys could have some semblance of their own lives. Keith and Kate would live in the larger house because of the influx of visitors they knew would come. Rachel would be away at work for days at a time and the boys would stay in the big house with their grandparents while she was in Houston. It sounded like a good plan.

The move from Houston was done with the blissful help of movers but when they left the place the mountainous job remaining was immediately overwhelming. The family began an extensive cleanup of the 52-acre haven they had found. Rachel, Elyse and Kate rolled up their sleeves, got out the scrub buckets and paintbrushes and the house began to smile.

Keith and the boys handled the outdoors with Madelyn (the youngest) Anderson helping. Fields were mowed, cleaned of debris and overgrowth, and trees were trimmed after long years of neglect. The ground was prepared for a vegetable garden, the fields were fertilized and seeded with hay and the farm was alive again.

The big friendly house had a huge kitchen with windows all along the wall on the south side. Kate decided it had possibilities. The room had wooden floors and two cook stoves. The wood burning stove would bake biscuits while heating the room at the same time on cold mornings.

The owners of the property had removed numerous walls from the original structure, as well as all of the windows on the east side of the kitchen….leaving nothing to stop the wind or weather other than a sun room with a hard plastic siding.

Two staircases made the upstairs accessible in a way that delighted the boys. The most decorative of the two was located in the living room. Kate had a sign posted halfway up the kitchen stairs that read "Beam me up Scotty." The possibility somehow comforted her.

The south Texas heat is notorious and so, like most sensible people, the Andersons had made certain that they had the benefit of air-conditioned homes for years. However, this one was cooled by nature, which did not do a very good job of it even though the house was breezy and fairly well insulated.

Sometimes, as she labored in the heat, sweat poured from her body and Kate wondered, "Whatever were we thinking?"

She and Rachel walked around covered with blotches of sea blue, egg shell yellow, raspberry pink, and baby blue paint in their hair and on their clothes. They stopped often and made fresh coffee, which they sipped together as they planned the decorating of the house. They made numerous runs into LaGrange, buying paint and selecting wall paper for the cottage. It was a wonderful happy time.

The three boys explored continually, often coming in with

scratches and bug bites, receiving the sympathy they wanted and then rushing off to see all that was to see in this new magical place. They were always warned, "Take a stick with you and watch for snakes." At night, all were searched for ticks and other hitchhikers they might have picked up during the day.

The stereo was usually playing James Taylor hits when Rachel was at home. Opera was Kate's favorite. Keith usually wanted to hear Merl Haggard or such and when Madelyn (the song bird) came home it was always a new tape with songs she was trying to learn for her appearances singing in restaurants and pubs in Houston. The mixture of choice was like the family, all different.

On occasion, Elyse came out from San Antonio and Madelyn from Houston to help with the work. Elyse (the Aggie of the clan) was expecting her first child at the time and she did not come often because of the heat that went unchecked with no air conditioning. She had married a boy from A & M, who was a Civil Engineer. They had met during their senior year there. Elyse was beautiful and considered "the quiet one" in the family. Her ash blond hair turned platinum in the summer sun. Her brown eyes gentle and kind, melted many male hearts. Her sisters called her the Judge and that was a suitable tag as well. She was the level headed, dependable one. The other three were not shy and often dared to go against their parents' wishes. Elyse kept the lid on things so to speak.

Madelyn was the most talkative, always laughing like her mom. Rachel was the older sister, the caretaker, and both were lively and fun to be around. Elyse was the quiet instigator of fun and trickery and had to be watched. Together, these three sisters were hilarious and kept everyone laughing even during the worst days. They were all beautiful. Madelyn - dark haired with her paternal grandmother's dark Spanish eyes (she was not Spanish but was always mistaken for such), had a glorious head of curly black (sometimes other colors) hair and high cheek bones which accented her large dark eyes. Rachel with long, silky strawberry blond hair, warm brown eyes, and lips most women would die for, was fair beyond description without a freckle on her light skin.

Kate always felt that no one could have had better daughters than these.

These three lively girls had been given creative gifts at birth and many projects were always in progress. Rachel never took her talent seriously but could paint or create anything asked of her in an instant. Only a suggestion would set her off and even the smallest request produced a surprising result. Kate once asked for a simple painting to cover an inside wall during a celebration at her church. It was to be water and some greenery. This became a 38 foot long 8 feet high mural that was truly beautiful. Huge cypress trees stood beside a lake which seemed to be somewhere in Louisiana with egrets, alligators, herons and a glorious sun setting behind the trees. It became a project so immense that Elyse added her gift of painting and the two sisters managed to complete the project just in time to be used for its original intent. Elyse was drawn into projects many times to help complete a simple task that had become too detailed and difficult under Rachel's hands.

When she began her nursing career, Rachel was assigned to Pediatrics and loved to entertain the children in her care. She drew funny pictures of her charges and told the children stories about themselves that she and Kate had written.

Instead of traditional nursing shoes, Rachel usually wore her tennis shoes and she wore them until the soles came loose, so loose that they had a flap in the front. When this happened the shoes were perfect for her purposes and she painted faces on the toes. These became puppets to make the children laugh. Wearing socks of the same color was not important to her and thus the characters on the toes of her tennis shoes were colorful individuals rather than a set.

The two younger sisters had busy lives elsewhere and most of the time Kate and Rachel were together. They had always been joined at the hip, or so the family said. They were inseparable and even when they were apart, the phone rang a dozen times a day going both ways with news of this or that. Usually, it was a movie on TV that Rachel knew her mother loved and she would make certain Kate didn't miss it.

Sometimes, Rachel, who was a lonely soul, called just to hear her mother's voice and calm down after some problem with her x spouse or something the boys needed. It was the same for Kate. Rachel was a good listener and during the years of Keith's illness, she could tell Rachel all of her feelings (anger, self-pity, sorrow) without being judged, no matter what those feelings were.

It was not unusual for Kate and Rachel to argue. Sometimes tempers flared (usually over something the boys needed discipline for) but these episodes would end as quickly as they began. On one occasion, the argument was going strong and Kate said, "Hey, you want a cup of coffee?" The conflict ended instantly and they were soon sitting at the kitchen table sipping on a fresh cup of their favorite brew, laughing and enjoying being together as they always had.

Chapter Five

What a way to begin

Texas is known for its oil for good reason. It seems to be everywhere. Obviously, there was a pool of it beneath this farm or in close proximity. Wherever oil exists, you will find sulfur. The smell of it was in the air and that odor was coming from the water pipes. Kate tried to not face the issue of the water immediately but to make the point clear to her, fate stepped in and the well broke down during the first day. Kate assured Keith that "that wasn't that much of a loss because the water stank profoundly of sulfur and was simply not potable anyway. " A cistern that stood on the west side of the house, squeezed in between the house and a dead tree full of honey bees, held enough rainwater for bathing but drinking water was purchased in town until a suitable filter could be found for the well. A second cistern stood near the barn and luckily, both were full.

The landlord reassured them that they "always drank the well water when they lived there". Kate doubted that. As far as she was concerned, that stuff could probably remove tooth fillings and kill warts with one swipe. A neighbor with the same water problem said

"Folks always stare at me in church after I've bathed."

The visit of the well man and his son and Kate's reputation

The well became a constant issue. Working only now and again and the well man made frequent visits. The one the Anderson's used was a middle aged man with a young son in his early twenties who came with him. On his first visit with his father, Kate and Rachel were painting somewhere in the house and in the heat, Kate had decided to wear a kerchief for a top and a pair of cutoff jeans. She had been raised to never appear in front of anyone outside of the family in such attire and so when the well man knocked on the door, she grabbed a large bath towel and held it in front of her as she stood on the screened porch and talked with him. His young son was standing behind him and Kate noticed that the blond haired, fair skinned young man was blushing and avoiding looking at her. His blue eyes were watering and she wondered what was wrong with him. When Kate and Rachel went back inside the house she mentioned his appearance and Rachel began laughing. "Mother, didn't you realize how you looked standing there with that towel? That boy thought you were naked." They both had a good laugh about that and the young man always blushed when he saw her after that day.

Kate received no comments on the subject but she had a feeling that her reputation had become a bit bent after the well man's visit.

．．．．．．．．．．．．．．．．．．．．．．．．．．．．．

While the family was settling in, Rachel was working in Houston taking care of Jim. Her patient was a night owl and seldom slept, so nights or days working made no difference. Her X spouse was a paramedic and worked 24 hour shifts so they had worked things out for her to stay at his apartment while he was away. This saved the cost of a place to stay over. The boys' dad paid his child support regularly but it was far from adequate and as far as Kate was concerned, this was the least he could and should do. Meanwhile, the three boys were under Kate and Keith's care ... and it was wonderful. The boys were ages 7, 5, and 2. With Aaron being the oldest, Sean in the middle and Patrick the youngest.

On the third day of their sojourn in their new home, Kate noticed Sean (age 5) looking rather perplexed as he stood on the front porch surveying the farm. He was the worrier of the family, often described as an old man in a boy's body. Kate hugged him and asked, "What's the matter, Sean? Aren't you happy here?" He assured her that he liked the farm but continued with his distressed expression. Once again she asked, "Well, then what's wrong?"

"I was just thinking about all of this work. I mean there's a lot to do. And I don't see how we're gonna do it. "In the end he finally explained his concerns about having to clean up the multitude of cow patties that surrounded the outside of the yard fence and indeed, the entire 52 acres. ... And whatever were "we going to do with all of it?" He was relieved to discover that the country was a different matter than city life with bugs, heat, and natural forces of nature helping considerably with unwanted refuse. It was easy to understand his first impression since Grandpa had a record of very grumpy relations with neighbors in the city who allowed their dogs to use his manicured front yard for a place to relieve themselves. Here, the cows had been much busier than those dogs and Sean thought all of those dried droppings had to be cleaned up. Once this project was marked off of the work list, Sean decided things were going to work out after all. A distasteful and exhausting daily scooping of the place would *not* be necessary.

Unpacking.......

Anyone who is familiar with country life knows that varmints of many varieties have to be dealt with. Fayette County had its share.

The first major assault came from fire ants, which took the family on in force. Those creatures obviously felt that they had first claim to the property and were well settled in in the house, yard, beds, walls, anywhere they wanted to be, and they wanted to be everywhere. They even maintained night sentries who lurked in the dark waiting for a crumb to fall.

It was that bad and anyone familiar with these guys knows that they were well organized.

During the unpacking phase, Rachel's three boys had to be warned constantly about the ants but they were still attacked often. Very alert scouts were obviously on duty because when one crumb hit the floor a line of ants immediately appeared to take care of the debris. If one of the boys forgot to look where he was going and stepped in the way of this work crew, a stinging armada covered him in an instant and made him pay for his mistake. Kate kept the rubbing alcohol close at hand along with cotton balls for the boys to rub their wounds so the adults could continue their work.

The boys helped by running back and forth bringing in buckets of water from the cisterns needed for all the scrubbing of everything in the house. They toted iced tea out to Grampa and Madelyn and carried messages when needed.

The place reeked of enamel, sulfa, human sweat, Pine Sol, insect spray and of course, rubbing alcohol.

The second discovery of "other inhabitants" in the house was a family of very large rats who also had no intentions of moving out.

Whenever possible, Madelyn (the youngest of the Anderson girls) came out from Houston to keep her finger in the pie on the farm. On one such occasion, she had elected to sleep on the couch in the living room. The rest of the family was sleeping upstairs at that time and had not realized that during the night the family of live-in rats celebrated the presence of a large bag of unshelled pecans located in the utility room by rolling the pecans all over the house. Kate had noticed pecans about the house in odd places but thought the boys had scattered them.

Somewhere after the house was quiet, Madelyn awoke to an unusually loud rattle. The next morning, Kate found her sleeping at the foot of one of the boy's beds upstairs. When asked why, Madelyn explained about the noise waking her, that of a hard shelled pecan rolling across the wooden floor. She soon realized that the sound was being produced by a very large rat who was taking his prize to parts unknown. "Mother, he was huge. That was the biggest rat I've ever seen. She said she threw a pillow in his direction. This guy was unafraid and continued to advance toward her. "He actually sat up and stared at me. It was like he dared me to throw another pillow, so I did. I threw one right at him and he just kept staring and rearing up and didn't move backward one whisker."

It quickly became evident that he might well decide to remove this upstart from the couch and even the room. Who was here first anyhow? Madelyn didn't need a house to fall on her and decided to not press the point. She headed for the safety of the family.

At the thought of a rat attack, Kate decided it was time for the rat family to go. Keith took care of the rats and a total of five were evicted with his efforts.

....

The discovery of the differences between town and country life provided numerous delights to all three of the male sprouts. First of all, they couldn't believe the profound joy of relieving themselves out in the open air.

Why hadn't they been TOLD that people could live like this?

One of their very favorite things was taking sidewalk baths. The first time they had one, they all frowned at the idea of bathing, *totally naked*, out in the open for all prying eyes to see, but then there were none around – so maybe it would be all right.

Their Grampa arranged the baths by gathering buckets of rainwater from the cistern, which was heated in a kettle by the smokehouse. The large iron kettle was set in a raised brick hearth, with a chimney on the south side. This was originally used when hogs and chickens were processed during the farm's beginnings. The smell of burning wood filled the yard and the boys were kept busy hauling water and bringing wood for the fire.

During the boys' sidewalk baths there was always squealing and giggling. Grampa usually ended up getting a bath with his clothes still on during the scrubbing. When this job was finished, Keith heated buckets of rain water from the cistern for Kate, hauling them inside with the delighted help of the boys … and filling the huge Jacuzzi tub for her bath. After a long hard workday, Kate's aching body soaked in this heavenly water and she considered how very wonderful her kind husband and his small assistants were. Sometimes it seemed to Kate, as if Keith was not ill and they were simply an exceptionally happy family. All things considered, they were and particularly the boys, who thought they had *"surely died and gone to heaven"*.

The view from the house was spectacular. The Fayetteville water tower was visible above the rolling green hills. Wildflowers bloomed in abundance everywhere and wild grapes and cattails lined the fencerows. Oak, pecan, crepe myrtle, red bud and numerous other trees added their splendor and the three ponds near the house reflected the beauty around them.

Even the nights were different. For Kate, years of life in the city had almost erased the memory of "so many" stars and now there they were in the same place they had been long ago. In the mornings, she woke to the view of dew glistening on the hills, the sound of trains passing through Fayetteville and the voices of roosters crowing on the neighboring farms.

She had the sense that the family had somehow traveled backward in time. The slower pace of this life was a blanket of calm that settled over her when she looked out across the hills or visited the little hamlet of Fayetteville. The tensions of Houston and the years of her husband's illness faded as she breathed in the wonder and beauty of the old yellow house and the green fields that surrounded it. She sometimes felt as if a storm had passed over and she was standing beneath a warm sun, watching the roaring clouds rolling away in the distance. She knew the winds could change, probably would, but for now, she was there in the calm regaining her strength to live again.

During the daylight hours when the work was done, the kids played on the tennis court or anywhere they wanted while every day without fail, their Grama watched Casablanca, her favorite movie. A fresh cup of coffee and Casablanca was her idea of heaven. She wrote songs and played her tunes on the piano and keyboard, or worked on her novel. She listened to the boys playing about the yard and the roosters who marched about as though each was the cock of the walk. Kate loved to hear them. They were a constant reminder that she was no longer encased in a brick house surrounded by city streets teeming with people.

Chapter Six

Trip to Cameron

Once the chicken house was cleaned and ready, Keith and Kate took the boys with them to Cameron to purchase baby chickens.

The boys were happy at the thought of hundreds of baby chickens and were up early. They ate a big breakfast and the five of them headed for Cameron. Kate and Keith were in the front seat of the suburban with the three boys strapped in in the back.

One of the problems with traveling with the boys had always been Patrick's motion sickness. Kate forgot about that in the excitement of their mission and so about half way to their destination, a groan from the back seat reminded her as Patrick announced, much too late, that he was going to upchuck. Before a cup or depository could be found, the proof of his problem surfaced - but the problem did not stop there.

At this "second sight" of Patrick's breakfast, the two other boys began losing theirs.

If three vomiting kids wasn't a problem, what was?

Keith quickly pulled to the side of the road and Kate jumped out to assist the boys. This was not a good move. With the abundance of places to stop, Keith had inadvertently chosen the armed camp of a hot tempered mob of fire ants. Kate was covered to the thighs with the angry things before she knew it and so the scene became complicated. Her hands were full of vomit and her pants were full of very unfriendly ants. A predicament she could not recall ever finding herself in before. Keith, the only one thinking clearly at this point, pulled the car away from the den of the beasts and Kate tried to remove the remaining live devils from her body and clothing.

She couldn't strip down here on a public road but the temptation and need to do so was intense.

Her legs were on fire now and the stench from the car was not too favorable either. It happened to be cold that morning but the back window of the suburban had to be lowered - if they wanted to breathe. The decision was to go on with the trip and pick up the new babies. Too high a price had already been paid anyway considering current events. The boys' problem had solved itself and they felt great by the time the chicks were placed in the car. On the way home, the chicks cheeped happily and the boys could not take their eyes or hands off of them. The fragrance of chicken poop mingled with the boys' soured breakfast in the floorboard and Kate hardly felt the cold air flowing freely in from the back window as she concentrated on the burning in her legs and feet.

She avoided looking at her husband as the slight smile on his face could easily have started an argument of huge proportions.

When Rachel was told about trip she regretted having missed it.

Chapter Seven

Rachel's patient

Actually, Rachel was missing a great deal and she knew it. She made good money in Houston; more than triple any wage she could receive in Fayetteville or LaGrange - making the long drive necessary for the support of her little family. Devoted to her boys, she also cared deeply for her patients – mostly infants and children with birth defects or terminal illnesses who had to be on respirators. She did not have the credentials, being an LVN, but because of her years of experience, she was considered a respiratory care specialist. This had led her to assignments with ALS patients and ultimately to Jim.

When Kate discovered that Rachel had been assigned to Jim Mitchell's case, she became concerned. Rachel was young, divorced, and Jim was only one year older.

This daughter who shared everything with her mother, asked for advice as she tried to understand her patient and make his life easier. He was still able to walk but had lost the use of his hands and arms, and was frequently falling. Still proud, he refused the use of his wheelchair.

In the beginning, Rachel resented the attitude of the angry young man but somewhere along the way, things began to change.

During the first year, she complained constantly about her moody patient being hard to please. She took few extra pains with her appearance and reluctantly waved goodbye to her children as she left the happiness of the farm for each two to three day work sequence. She had a tremendous weight on her shoulders with being a single parent to her sons and there was clearly an added danger in this situation. Nature has its way with the young and falling in love with a man who had a terminal illness wasn't going to help the situation.

It would be a disaster. Kate warned against "caring too much for Jim".

Each time, her remarks were met with scoffs from Rachel and a reminder that her patient was, after all, a married man.

Rachel's words describing the beginning of their relationship.........

Far from being a match made in heaven, or love at first sight; it was a long shot that Jim and I would be able to build more than a casual acquaintance. I was apprehensive about meeting him when I learned that I was being assigned to his case....nurses gossip among themselves, and I had heard him described at different times as cute, mischievous, intelligent, opinionated, impossible.... No matter how wonderful the description had been up to a point, it was apparently the general consensus that he was difficult to handle. By the time I had worked with him a few months I had decided that for once the nurses had been overly charitable. When he was on a roll, he could be an incredible asshole; stubborn beyond belief, rude, superior, etc. Although he jokingly called himself The Grand Monarch and Overseer of the Universe, I came to believe that if the truth were known, he actually saw himself in that capacity – his name on the door, the Big O. I discovered later that he had dismissed me as being a disorganized dingbat, and although he would flirt and pass the time with idle banter, he was simply indulging his propensity for manipulating females in general. He admitted; once he felt our relationship was strong enough to survive the candor that just about anything I said to him on any subject, went in one ear and out the other.

In all fairness, I deserved the dingbat label. I have never mastered some of life's simpler chores. I cannot balance a checkbook, and I am one of the few people that manage better by estimating their balance, because my math is usually wrong but my estimates are occasionally correct. I would make endless lists of things I needed to do, but I could never find the list. I am also opinionated, stubborn, and hot tempered, so the possibility exists that I was actually frustrated that I had encountered someone capable of outmaneuvering me in a battle of wills.

Despite all of this, Jim and I managed to avoid any confrontations or bruised feelings because other than the nursing care that he required, we stayed out of the others way for the most part. As time passed, we realized that we did share some common interests - an addiction to the original Star Trek series, a love of animals and any food with absolutely no nutritional value, and collecting useless trivia. Jim could stump you on obscure information on an amazingly wide variety of subjects, and if he was making it up as he went along, which I often suspected him of doing, it was impossible to call him on it because he was willing to argue the point until you gave in out of exhaustion. My area of expertise was limited, but because I had been a night-owl since childhood, I was an encyclopedia of movies and actors all the way back to the 30's. It became a contest, and if I drew a blank on the names of the original Mercury astronauts, my revenge came in asking him to give me the name of the actress who played Johnny Weissmuller's Jane, or the Ricardo's apartment number.

Tolerance became a grudging respect, and at some point we both began to look forward to the days that I would work with him. I continued to wait for a signal from him that he wanted to talk, or company while he watched a movie, because I came to realize that the pre-illness Jim had apparently been extremely independent, a man who enjoyed a certain amount of solitude, and that independence was trapped in an increasingly dependent body. He was forced to weigh every word for fear that either false hope or resignation would be read into them. He couldn't go off by himself any longer, not when he was incapable of opening a door, or even walking unaided.

Instead of being a perpetual snit about it all, which I'm afraid my reaction would have been, his sense of humor seemed to grow stronger. Awkward, painful moments were salvaged by Jim himself, comforting those around him. I would see the pain in his face as he caught a glimpse of himself in the mirror,- his arms and *shoulders growing thinner, his muscles melting away, to have him look up at me with a smile, cautioning me that I would have to control my sexual frenzy in the presence of such male perfection. He began to drop his guard when we talked and I realized that his arrogance and exasperating stubbornness were the extremes of strength and resolution. The long periods of silence, broken only with terse requests for nursing care, were the times when his strength had been tapped, and rather than giving in to the depression and frustration, Jim withdrew, focusing everything he had on regaining control.*

Rachel

During these months of their growing knowledge of one another, Jim was finally forced into a wheelchair after a nasty fall sent him to the hospital emergency room. Rachel became very upset when she heard the news of the fall.

Kate observed that reaction with an uneasy feeling in the pit of her stomach.

Her concern grew when she learned that Jim's wife had begun dating other men, going out and leaving her husband completely alone at night when the nurses were not on duty. Sometimes, Jim waited until three or four a.m., needing someone to help him to the bathroom.

Rachel watched his pain as he fought the disease and helplessly withstood his wife's neglect and infidelity. Obviously, the woman had difficulty dealing with what was happening to Jim and their marriage but to someone like Rachel, that woman's behavior was unforgivable.

Warning flags really began to fly in her second year of caring for Jim when Rachel began to wash and fluff her long strawberry blond hair to a high gloss, overwork her makeup, and ask extensive questions about which blouse and tight blue jeans looked best before leaving for Houston.

Things rocked on for a while before the last straw fell. That came when Jim's wife laid down beside him and tried to commit suicide. She was in pain – that was understandable but this was punishing him for being ill. He could do nothing. Thankfully, she was discovered in time and was not successful in her attempt. Shortly thereafter, this wife told Jim to go to Galveston and live out the remainder of his life with his family. This move was to end Rachel's assignment of caring for him.

Chapter Eight

The hills of Fayette County

Following his last day in Houston, Rachel came home, obviously extremely upset. She was usually overjoyed to see her boys after being away, but this time she needed some time away from the clamor of her children. Kate looked at her face and knew what to do. She took her daughter for a long quiet drive through the hills of Fayette County. Rachel poured out her anger and frustration at Jim's wife for what she was doing to him and Kate listened. They drove by a small church with a cemetery beside it, set high on a hill in the open countryside. Rachel began to cry and asked, "Mother, do you realize just how many people whom I have come to love are in a place like this?" Kate knew. She also knew Rachel was telling her that she could not bear the thought of never seeing Jim again.

They cried together in that quiet place on a hill. No words could change what was to come. A mockingbird began its trill nearby. Even his efforts could not lift Rachel's heart. When the tears were done, they drove home in silence to the arms of her sons. The boys saw their mother's face and looked at Kate as if to say, "Did you make Mama cry?" Kate said, "Your mama needs your hugs. That's what she needs." They gave them freely and Kate watched as they went together to their cottage. Kate would prepare dinner and life would go on.

As she had feared, Rachel had fallen in love with the brilliant young man who had become her friend. She knew they had had long talks and Jim had done the one thing a woman cannot resist. He had bared his soul to her.

Jim went to Galveston and Rachel waited to see if he would forget her.

Phone calls for Rachel.....

During this time, visitors came to the farm in droves to see what Kate and Keith had "*gotten themselves into*" but the Andersons were exactly where they wanted to be. Even with all of the hard work over the past months, Kate loved the farm and the big kitchen more than any other part of the house.

The windows above the cabinet top were always filled with fresh vegetables from the garden or eggs from her very own hens. She cooked constantly and Rachel's boys usually crowded about her feet wanting to know "What's for dinner, Grandma." From this happy room, Kate began answering phone calls from Jim.

The phone began to ring more and more. Kate answered to a soft male voice asking for Rachel in words slurred and apologetic. Sometimes Rachel cried after talking to him, other calls left her beaming.

The long distance friendship developed into trips to Galveston where she loaded Jim into his wheelchair and took him out to restaurants (where they often "closed down the joint"), evenings sitting on the beach, and other private moments. He was not to be allowed to hide away from life. She made him see that other people didn't matter, and he began to believe that all was not finished for him after all.

Jim's letter to Rachel....try to understand how I feel...
December 1989..

Dear Rachel,

I decided that it would be a good idea if I tried writing to you to try to make you understand how I feel. Every time we talk about certain things, I always feel that I didn't do a very good job of communicating my feelings to you. I sometimes feel uneasy and incomplete after we talk, like something important was left out. It's not you, it's me. I don't do well explaining how I feel.

A year ago, I had resigned myself to moving to Galveston and living out the rest of life there. Getting involved with someone, and getting married were the farthest things from my mind. Then I started seeing you. Well sweetheart, you know the story, and you also know that I'm not proud of the way I treated you in the beginning.

Rachel, you showed me that it is okay to go

ahead and love someone even though I have ALS. Then you taught me that I should not be afraid to live my life like I was normal, and that included taking on the responsibility of having a family. I wonder sometimes if you realize the impact that all of this has had on me. I am still very much afraid that I will put you and the boys through unnecessary pain. I don't want to be a burden on you and especially on the boys. I know you disagree but please understand, I can't help but feel that way.

What you have done for me is very hard to put into words. You have given me what I thought could never be again. You have offered me three wonderful sons that I can only hope to be able to raise. To top it off, you have given me a kind of love that I have never known. Every other relationship that I've had is nothing compared to what I have with you. If you could live off of the emotion that pours out of my heart for you, you would never be sick, tired, hungry, thirsty, and you would never lack for anything.

I do not know why we argue the way we do. Maybe it's frustration, or maybe we are impatient for the life we don't have. I don't know, but I do know that whatever we have ahead of us, I can handle it. I am so much in love with you that I am willing to do anything to make it work. I don't want to live without you. I'm not feeding you a line either. It probably sounds like it, but I'm not. Surely, you know that by now.

You told me a couple of times that I have said things to you that some women only dream about hearing. Well, the same is true for me. I only thought that I had experienced the best that life had to offer. After being with you, I now realize that you are what I have been waiting and looking for. Being with you has been the best time of my life. I can't believe how lucky I am to have you and the boys.

Jim

Chapter Nine

Jim's narrative.......ALS

Light Years excerpts from Jim's unfinished work

I suppose I could begin with when I was born and fill these pages with all of the good of my normal life. I won't do that.

I think the beginning of 1985 would be the best place to start because it was the beginning of the beginning. That was the point where my second life began.

January of 1985 was the first touch of the insidious thing that I have been fighting. It was like a tap on my shoulder. I turned and nothing was there. It was that slight and so I ignored it, filed it away like a toe stumped on a small bump in the road. These symptoms were trying to tell me something but I did not realize they were symptoms, just odd things happening to me.

Almost eighteen months passed before the happenings became obvious enough for me to take action and find out what was going on.

It is not significant to describe my life at that time. I was a normal guy. I worked for an electrical company and was doing alright financially. I was very athletic and regularly played basketball, tennis, swam and surfed in the ocean in Galveston Bay or any other active thing guys enjoy.

I experienced what I now believe to be the first symptom as I was going down a flight of stairs. I noticed that my feet were not as coordinated as they should be. The usual 1-2 cadence eluded me. I went back up the stairs and tried again and again to make it right but to no avail. The last move I made was to trip and fall at the bottom. I made excuses for myself, out of shape etc. or I was having a bad day. I filed it away in the back of my head. I should have known better and in retrospect I see that I should have listened to my body.

Another symptom was my inability to jump as high as I had been able to do earlier. I ignored it. Other things were hitting me at this point. I began to have unusual cramping in my neck when I held the phone on my shoulder. My arms became increasingly heavy when I reached over my head and the most obvious symptom was the twitching of the muscles in and around my shoulders. The twitching began in the latter part of 1984 but did not become a constant irritation until June of 1986. The insidious thing was working on my body and I was ignoring it.

The twitching would last about five minutes, stop for a while and then start over again. After a few days of this, I began hitting myself trying to make it go away. I tried stretching, twisting, scratching, pulling, and even pinching but nothing seemed to help.

People would come to my desk and ask what the heck I was doing.

Strangely enough, I was still not, would not be, alarmed.

My weakness grew and my frustration with it. I lost at basketball to guys who had never even played the game before, almost drowned several times and completely stalled out when I tried to dive from a cliff into the ocean. Cold temperatures and being bumped or touched sometimes sent me into one of those stall outs.

My speech was not the same. When I had a few drinks my words were slurred as if I had had far too many. Things were piling up.

I always enjoyed my coffee and I began to notice that I couldn't get from the coffee pot to my desk without spilling, no matter how careful I was.

In May of 1986 my wife and I went on a Caribbean Cruise to Haiti, Jamaica, the Cayman Islands, and Cozumel, Mexico. This was our sixth trip,

I knew by now that there was something wrong with me, I just didn't know what. Deep down inside, warning lights and sirens were going off but I kept shoving the whole idea of being ill down into a place where I would think about it later.

Other abilities began to fall. I had trouble writing, I became lethargic about anything that *required physical exertion and after a hard fall while playing basketball, I had stopped playing altogether.*

I rationalized that an injury five years earlier and the surgery to repair the muscles and tendons had messed me up causing weakness and possibly had effected my entire muscular system.

A number of incidents happened on that last vacation that took me down. I fell during a climb up a waterfall and almost drowned while snorkeling because I could not control my breathing. I had "lived "in the water most of my life and this was "not happening".

I had a memorable discussion with my friend David, where we went over possibilities of what might be wrong with me. The bottom line was that everything we came up with, we assumed was fixable. It did not occur to me that my problem might not be curable or that it might be terminal. My life had become full of could be's and what if's.

By July of 1986, the problem had become so obvious that I was forced to take action.

The twitching in my upper body had grown worse, my hands were becoming more awkward every day, any exertion left me exhausted, and my speech was beginning to slur. I was tired of the speculation about my plight. I went to see our family doctor.

Our family doctor was an older man with a lifetime of experience. We were fond of him and trusted him. He was extremely thorough in his examination. I spent about 45 minutes in his office. He seemed particularly concerned about my eyes, running all kinds of tests on them. I became very nervous and asked him why. Apparently, when exploring possible nerve disorders, a problem with the eyes indicates one thing. If the eyes are okay, then something else is indicated. At the time, it made little sense to me. I was just relieved that there was nothing wrong with them, or so I thought.

All during the exam, I had been describing the symptoms I had been having in as much detail as possible and he had been asking questions.

When he was finished, he sat down, looked me straight in the eyes, and said that he felt that I had some kind of sclerosis. He could not tell me exactly what kind it was, but he wanted me to go see the neurologist and find out.

I was confused. First, I knew that our family doctor was good, but I was unwilling to accept what he had told me. He could be wrong. Second, I found it very hard to believe that something as serious as a kind of sclerosis could be the problem. It would be almost a month later that I would find that my doctor was not only right: he had hit the nail right on the head.

My own physician, recommended a friend of his who was at Baylor College of Medicine in Houston but I decided to go home to Galveston and see someone there. The University of Texas Medical Branch was located there and my parents still lived in Galveston. I felt more at home in Galveston and we knew people in the medical community who could help us locate the very best neurologist available.

On August 12, 1986, a Monday morning, my mom and I were scheduled in to see the head of neurology at John Sealy Hospital in the Medical Center. This was crunch time, and I have to admit, I was damn nervous. It was fourth and goal with time running out, and I didn't have a play to run. I was out of excuses and this time, whatever it was, we would know and we would deal with it.

I went through a duplicate of the tests my family doctor had given me only a lot more extensively. The first thing he asked me to do was walk. Looking back, I realize that right then, he knew exactly what I had. Even now, when I am at clinic, I can watch the way that a new patient is walking and tell if he or she has the same illness. That was not an easy day. Truthfully, I was worrying about my mother and my family, more so than for myself. I would have given anything to be able to protect them from what might be.

Following that office visit, I had to check into the hospital for more tests. He gave Mom the hope that there might be a cyst on my spinal cord. The only way to find out was more testing. He also said he was looking for a place on my spine where something, anything could be exerting pressure.

Hospitals are cold and the beds uncomfortable but if I had to be in one at all, John Sealy was the one I would have chosen. My room was on the 9th floor and from my window I could see part of the beach and the eastern half of Galveston.

First test was an MRI. The technicians put me on the platform and strapped me down and I thought, "Well, this is odd." I had looked at the machine and there was no way I could fall off the platform. What was it going to do, buck me off? They finished tucking me in and then they both walked out of the room and shut the door. So I lay there thinking "what now?" When they finally began the procedure I had become sleepy. A voice at my side told me to try to be still. I was not alone after all.

The starting and stopping of the hammering sound of that machine went on for an hour and a half. I felt that it was not so bad overall but when they came the next day and told me they would have to do it again I was not too happy. As it turned out, the second session was a lot shorter than the first and went a lot smoother. The technician gave me a Polaroid picture of my brain from this day's work.

An EMG followed to measure the conductivity of nerves in one of my arms. In other words, they were going to give me some electrical shocks. For someone whose nerves were supposedly not functioning properly, mine seemed to work fine that day.

From there other tests came which included needles in my skin, twenty or thirty sticks in each arm and leg with my back receiving its fair share. My chin and tongue were not left out and when this was all over I went to my room so tired that I felt like I had died.

A group of young interns, seven or eight, came into my room and did their part of the testing, using me as a guinea pig. When one of them began putting on rubber gloves I informed them that I had no problem with my prostate gland and that was the end of that.

At 12:30 P.M. on August 14, 1986, Dr. Johnson walked into my room, pulled a big chair close to the bed and sat down. My heart was racing and I could almost feel my blood pressure going up. I knew this was it. Suddenly, I wasn't sure that I wanted to hear what I was about to be told. I took a few deep breaths, forced myself to relax and turned to face the inevitable.

The curable things he was looking for, the cyst, etc. were not there. The MRI had found no abnormalities but the EMG proved that the nerves were not working properly. He said, "You have a motor neuron disease." He went on to explain that the upper motor neurons in my body were not functioning as they should and my muscles were deteriorating. The name of the beast surfaced for the first time. He called it amyotrophic lateral sclerosis (ALS). He continued explaining the prognosis which was three to five years of life with no known cure. I asked if there was a layman's term for this disease. It all hit home when he said, "Lou Gehrig's Disease".

I had stood up and moved to the other side of the bed. My legs turned to rubber and I sat down on the bed. The doctor stayed and talked to me explaining what I could expect and after I assured him that I was okay, he left me there alone.

The first thing I thought about was my family. Goodness knows I had had plenty of warning that this news was coming, almost six months. I wasn't completely surprised. The next question in my mind is probably a universal one in these circumstances..."Why me?" As I sat there mulling over all of the doctors words, it suddenly occurred to me that if anyone in my family had to get a serious illness, it should be me. I was the oldest, big brother, and all that. If I had a good, positive attitude from the very beginning, it would make everything easier for everyone. I decided I would keep my head no matter what.

It was time now to tell the family

I called Mom, told her that Dr. Johnson was releasing me that afternoon and asked her to come and get me. When she asked, I had to tell her. It was the hardest thing I've ever had to do. That evening, all of my family got together, and we shared our feelings about what had happened and was going to happen. I could not have made it without them.

My family had not known about any of the symptoms that had been plaguing me and so the diagnosis was much more of a shock to them than it was to me.

ALS is a bizarre disease. No two people are affected in the same way and this makes things harder to deal with in the beginning. There are two forms of ALS. One is called bulbar and the other progressive. Bulbar ALS affects the throat, mouth, and the lungs. Progressive affects the remainder of the body. Since I had already had problems speaking, I had to assume that I had bulbar involvement. Unfortunately, I also had been having problems with my hands and arms, which meant I had progressive as well. This was just great. Not only did I have ALS, I had both types of it. It was like getting a ticket for a broken headlight, and then on the way to get it fixed, getting another ticket.

I stayed in Galveston for another week, not wanting to face friends and associates at work or elsewhere right away. The only thing I had given serious thought to was my attitude. My work did not include a lot of heavy lifting or physical things so I decided to go back to work, at least for the time being. Long term thought or planning was out of the question but I wasn't laying down either.

Throughout the fall of 1986, my symptoms became steadily worse until Thanksgiving of 1986. After that holiday and the opportunity to talk things over with my family, I decided I would quit trying to work at the end of the year.

I knew I was on my way to success in my job but everything I thought was to be flew out the window and I had to step back and reassess where I was going in the time remaining. The only thing I knew for certain was that my first job was going to be to maintain the right attitude, a positive one that believed a future existed for me and even the possibility of being cured of ALS.

The phrase, you find out who your friends are took on a new meaning for me. At first, everyone was sympathetic and understanding but as the symptoms became more obvious, people's attitude towards me began to change.

It began with a lack of things in common. Since I had quit work because my hands couldn't hold a pen properly, I discovered that socially, I didn't have anything to talk about with my friends, namely work. I found myself doing a lot more listening than I was accustomed to and I learned how much our world revolves around our jobs. The major thing was, most of my friends did not want to talk about my illness. Many people wouldn't look me in the eye. Those who did would usually say something like, "I'm so sorry this is happening to you," or the worst "Now don't let this get you down." I felt so angry but the truth is, there was nothing they could say. It was one of those damned if you do and damned if you don't situations.

I actually was naïve enough to think that my illness wouldn't make a difference to my friends. I figured maybe a couple of them wouldn't be able to handle my having a terminal illness, but I was completely wrong. I had the numbers right but turned around. There were a couple of them, but they were the ones who could handle my illness. Almost all of my friends quit coming around. By the time the disease forced me into a wheelchair, only three of my friends came to visit regularly and one was a new friend that I met after my diagnosis. Out of twenty to thirty friends, there was only one person who had the courage to tell me that they couldn't handle my being sick and that I would probably not see much of them.

Chapter Ten

Lost work

There are many chapters of Jim's work on Light Years missing. I will include here a portion of Chapter seven which was in some of the records I have found and collected. Three pages are missing but there is much of the flavor of his work here, and best of all, his feelings about Rachel.

....

When I was growing up, Mike and I shared the upstairs room at our house in Galveston. In June of 1989 when I had to move back to Galveston, I would have liked to move back into the same room. Unfortunately for me, this was not possible. Mom and Buddy were now using the upstairs for their bedroom, and even if they weren't I couldn't get up the stairs anyway. Our house is a duplex, with Grandmother living in the other half. Her bedroom and the room I was going to be in opened onto a patio that both houses shared. It's too bad that I couldn't walk anymore because I would have had easy access to seeing Grandmother whenever I wanted.

The things that I brought with me from Houston barely fit into my new room. My computer, TV, stereo, a dresser, and a bookcase took up most of the room. Mom and Buddy bought me a day bed and that was all we could squeeze in. It must have looked a little strange with all of my posters on the walls. They had been located in my computer room in Houston, a room that most visitors never saw. Here, it was all out in the open. We had everything arranged so that I could work the TV and stereo with my foot and one knee. The entertainment center Mike gave me made it possible for the buttons on the cable box to be at knee level.

Everything was going fine, I was all moved in and knew that I would be happy in Galveston. There were a few inconveniences. First, the only way to get into the house was up some stairs. The front door had the curb and four stairs. The patio had two big steps and a sliding glass door that was impassable for my wheelchair. Then there was the bathtub. The tubs in both houses were sunken. It was impossible for me to lift myself out after bathing even with assistance. Buddy came up with the idea to build a monorail system on the ceiling. This would go from my room all the way to the bathroom. Until then, I would have to take sponge baths.

Entering the house was solved by Buddy and his friend building a deck on the patio. The deck was a ramp that ran all the way to the street. When the sliding doors were replaced with regular doors I could go in and out whenever I wanted. They solved the shower problem with a few more clever moves and I was all set.

My social life took a hit when I went to Galveston. I loved staying up late at night and here I had to go to bed around ten-thirty. Mike and Valerie came over often and we tried to go out to movies and things. Life wasn't the same but it was better than it had been with that other woman. The only thing I missed was not having my step daughter around. I missed not having my own home anymore. I knew I had to move because of the way Pat was behaving but it was hard for me to give up all that I had worked so hard for. I had left most of the things we had collected during our married life with her. I thought I had to do the right thing and to me that meant taking only what I needed.

In the third week of July, I found out I had been a blockhead. I heard via the grapevine that my wife had a new roommate and it was a guy. I was furious, mostly at myself for being so stupid. This woman had been complaining to me for six months about how hard things were on her. She had said over and over that it was "her time", meaning time for her to enjoy life and not work so hard. I had given her my social security money so she wouldn't have to worry and she had stabbed me in the back. She was unstable. Her suicide attempt proved that but she wasn't that bad off and this was the last straw.

When I met this woman, she was nothing. Now, she had a very successful job and because I was gone, things were looking up for her. She was a taker and she had taken me, but good.

I felt as though my privacy had been invaded. That was still my house she was living in with this man. If that woman had never taken in her new roommate, there's no telling how long I would have gone on before my anger came out. I had thought I was in love with her but looking at her from a distance I realized that I was never really in love with her. For the first time since my diagnosis, I became depressed. My family came to the rescue as always.

I let the depression take hold for about two weeks, visible to everyone but it actually controlled me for about two months.

Our money situation was one of the main problems. I had allowed her to control the money, even having to ask for funds when I needed them. By the end of July, I was messed up, confused, depressed, and questioning what on earth I had done with my life anyway. All of the recent eye openers had taken three years to hit me on the head. Why had it taken me so long to see what everyone else had seen years ago?

There were other things going on in my life that were upbeat and positive. I became involved at the clinic with a group of ALS patients. I was a big part of that and my entire family took part as well. We had a group called Always Lending

Support. That' name explains the purpose. We were all in this together, trying to help one another.

Whenever I think about my illness, I feel a determination in me that forces me to be positive. Any time I get down, I concentrate on ALS and feel the attitude in me. I feed off of it.

One of my favorite things about being in Galveston was my relationship with my mother. I've always been very close to my grandmother, but with Mom, it was different. We didn't always see eye to eye on things but we still shared a special kind of relationship. She can bring me up when I'm down and vice-versa. We spent very special time together and it was the same with the rest of my family. There were more weekends with Mike and Valerie and we started doing things together more often.

We were all doing new things, Mike going into politics, Val teaching writing, and myself deciding to write poetry, something I had never done before. Even with all of this, I would have been in big trouble except for something unexpected that happened making me one of the luckiest men alive.

It was a simple mutual attraction that brought Rachel and I together, yet it had started with friendship. During my last days in Houston, Rachel and I had become very close. It was unusual because we didn't talk about what was happening to me. We talked about each other and the fact that we wanted to be together. We were good friends, No, we were more than just good friends but because she was one of my nurses we never had a chance for anything more. After we started dating around mid-July, I know that some of our friends were probably thinking and saying that we had been "carrying on" while Rachel was my nurse, and I feel sorry for them. People seem to like to think the worst, and in Rachel's case with the other nurses, I sensed some jealousy for whatever reason.

Rachel and I were brought up by parents who for the most part, did things the old fashioned way. That, plus the fact that we were both products of the seventies, the last true decade of drugs, sex, rock-n-roll, which meant that we had been through all of the wild crazy stuff and it was out of our system. Now, we had some of the old-fashioned morals and values instilled by our parents.

In Houston, Rachel had a career that was vital to her survival and she would do nothing to jeopardize that and, I still had a wife which was a major factor. That kept me from jumping Rachel's bones. (I just wanted to say that).

Okay, so we dated after I went to Galveston and I was still legally married at that time. Legally was the only aspect of being married as nothing else existed or was going to be from that point on.

The most remarkable thing about our relationship was that neither of us looked for it or expected it to happen. In the spring of 1989 when I realized that I would have to move out of my home in Houston, I believed that I would live the remainder of my life in Galveston. I also thought I would never have a relationship with a woman again. What woman would want a dieing man? There was no future in it. Rachel, on the other hand, did not have the fear that some women have after a divorce, mainly the fear of not having a man around for support. Her marriage had been a strain on her and her three sons. *She wasn't going to go through that again. She made a good living on her own and didn't need a man to support her. So, the fact that we began seeing each other was pretty incredible.*

Getting to know her made the difference for me. First I knew her as my nurse and I took her for granted. I didn't take the time to really get to know her. Other nurses, whom I now realize had some jealousy behind their words, talked against her. I listened in the beginning and I'm not proud of how I treated her during those early days. I dismissed things she said like she didn't know what she was talking about.

We started dating because we wanted to and because we were attracted to each other. We had a lot in common, we laughed together and we had been and still were good friends. Besides, Rachel is a slim, beautiful blond and more to my liking. I don't know why I ever married "that woman" for a number of reasons, one of those being that she was a brunette.

At home, when I was alone, my thoughts were confused to say the least. I really wanted to have a relationship with Rachel but everything inside of me said not to do it. It wasn't right. I should not become involved with anyone because of my ALS. The reasons were obvious. It wouldn't be fair to Rachel and my future had no promise whatsoever. I had to do the right thing, for both of us. I told myself this over and over, yet, come August I was still seeing her. A psychiatrist would have had a field day with me.

Our relationship had its limitations. I was at Rachel's mercy as far as when we could see each other. She was working at night as a critical care nurse, usually working with patients on ventilators, plus she was raising three boys, and she lived way out in the sticks. She usually left work, which was in or around Houston, drove 120 miles home to Fayetteville to spend a few hours with her sons, and then she would drive another three hours to Galveston to see me. Looking back, I feel very guilty about what she went through to see me.

The weekends we had together are something I will always cherish. I would never trade them for anything. Rachel is a very special kind of woman. To do all of that and put up with me is unbelievable.

If someone asked me how I felt about her, I'm not sure what my answer would have been. I know that I loved her, but I had not thought about whether I was in love with her. I thought I didn't want to be in love with anyone. That attitude seriously affected the way I treated her. She always said, "It's okay with me, I'll take whatever we have and be happy." I suppose I have to admit that confusion had control of me more than level headed thinking.

By this time, I had decided that someone else needed to start running the meetings of the Always Lending Support group. People were having difficulty understanding me when I talked, so in May I announced that I was resigning as chairman. I still attended the meetings and took over writing the newsletter.

During the summer of 1989, my brother Mike made the decision to run for state representative from Galveston. We had all known since he was about ten years old that he wanted to go into politics so his decision was no surprise.

As always, my thoughts return to Rachel.

In July I was confused about her but that didn't

stop me from continuing to see her. To be honest, I couldn't get enough of her. On Thursday and Friday of a week that I knew she was coming on the weekend, I was fidgety and anxious. On the day she was to arrive, I was probably unbearable. She had a tendency to run later than expected and I would be crazy by the time she arrived. Love will make you do strange things and I was finally willing to admit that I loved Rachel.

By October, things had changed dramatically. I had my head together. I wasn't confused about anything anymore. The "other woman" was out of my life. Without a doubt I was happier in Galveston than I had been in Houston. I had a girlfriend, who for some reason was crazy about me and I was kind of nuts about her. My attitude could not have been better and I felt like I was holding my own with the ALS.

It was time for me to do some heavy thinking about what direction I wanted to take with my life. The idea of not spending the rest of my days in Galveston was beginning to tease me a little.

Mom was the first one to become aware of what was developing between Rachel and I. I talked often with Mom about Rachel and what was happening between us. I expressed my skepticism about having a relationship. I don't remember who was the first to say it, Mom or Rachel, but I know it was about the same time when they both began telling me that it was okay for me to be with Rachel. They both said I shouldn't be afraid of going farther with our relationship because of my illness. It was a matter of "getting on with my life, not giving up, and trying to live a normal life."

I had told myself when I gave up and moved to Galveston that that was it, no more woman, no more relationships, no more marriage, and no more sex. I wouldn't call that a positive attitude but I still didn't know what the heck to do. However, I continued seeing Rachel, knowing full well that I was getting in deeper and deeper and very aware that I might end up hurting her.

Rachel started telling me about this house in Fayetteville that she really liked. I was immediately suspicious. This was a conspiracy and I wasn't falling for it. I began to pull away from her. Oh no, there was no way she would ever convince me to move to Fayetteville with her, absolutely not. If, by some wild chance we ended up together, it would be in Galveston. I told her that it would really be a shot in the dark if we ever got together. That was something way off in the distance and a very big if. She just smiled and told me it was okay. She wasn't asking for any kind of commitment. She just liked this house a lot and was thinking about renting it.

By the end of October, I had learned another lesson. Actually, it was two lessons but they're along the same lines. I learned that I didn't have to stop living a somewhat normal life just because I was living with my parents. I had lost my home in Houston but that didn't mean that I had to quit on life in general. Rachel had proved me wrong about the girlfriend thing and there were a lot of things I could still do. This woman had proven to me that I could have any kind of relationship I wanted with the right person. Although what she saw in me still eludes me.

When Thanksgiving came, I was at a loss without Rachel there, moping around while everyone else had a good time. I began to face what was going on inside of me about Rachel but I was still not admitting anything to anyone else. I knew that I loved her but I was still trying to do the right thing.

My health had remained relatively stable throughout that year. The one thing that seemed to worsen was my speech which alternated between almost normal to barely understandable.

By December, things were pretty good for me. I was happier than I had been in a long time and my attitude was great. Rachel had made her decision about the house in Fayetteville and told me it would take a mountain of work to make it livable. I feigned apathy about the whole house thing. I was not going to Fayetteville.

When I contemplated my situation honestly I found that I was a bit perturbed that Rachel had taken the matter of where we might live out of my hands. She had rented that house so she wouldn't be coming to Galveston. If I wanted her, I would have to go to the sticks. Oh heck, I was right back to my July confusion.

This caused the first misunderstanding between my new love and I. We were talking on the *phone one day, once again discussing the house. She asked what I was going to do as far as she and I were concerned. Was there anything special she should do to the house in case I moved up there? My thoughts had been that if there was any new development that it would happen about six months down the road. Instead of explaining or admitting my confusion, I became defensive and angry with her. I didn't like the pressure. I told her if she needed a decision right then she could do whatever she wanted to that house but to count me out. I think that must have been one of those times Kate says Rachel cried after talking to me on the phone.*

It was sometime in the middle of January when Rachel came to see me for another weekend. I had made up my mind about all of it and asked her to marry me or we agreed on what we both wanted. I don't remember all that was said. Over the Christmas holidays I had done a lot of thinking and plenty of talking with my family. They had assured me that I should do whatever I wanted and if I wanted to be with Rachel, then that's what I should do. I was feeling better about everything in my life. I felt as if I were becoming my old self again.

Rachel was concerned that I might be on the rebound from my first marriage. I had discovered that my feelings for Rachel were so intense that I could not even remember having felt anything for that other person. The whole subject was no longer important.

The last question between us was where we were going to live.

Remember, I said I was not going to Fayetteville? Guess where I was moving. Rachel and her boys could not, would not move to Galveston. She had lived there before and didn't like it. If my family had not been there, I would've had no reason to like it either.

And so our final planning began. We would have to have nurses there while Rachel was at work but that changed when we received a letter from Blue Cross of Rhode Island. My health insurance was under the group plan of the company I had worked for. We discovered that since February would mark three years since my diagnosis, Blue Cross was now going to only provide health insurance under an individual plan which *amounted to no coverage of any value. I was going to have to pay the premiums for this. The plan was transferred to Texas. The end result was that I was no longer covered for nursing care. Mike had warned me this could happen a few years earlier. I did not look forward to giving this news to Rachel. Whatever we did, we would have to manage without nursing care. It was my mom who came to the rescue. She reminded me that this did not have to be the end of Rachel and I. In fact it changed nothing for us because I had to have nursing care. Whether I lived in Galveston or Fayetteville, I would still have to have it. We had to look at this thing like any other budget, figure our expenses and see where we had to go from there. Once again, I became excited at the prospect of moving to Fayetteville and getting married. I would be with my Rachel. That was the most important thing.*

Jim's notes ended here. There were more but what happened to them, no one knows. Pages were missing and small segments remained in Rachel's files after his death. Hopefully, enough of his personality is here for the reader to see our Jim.

Chapter Eleven

The Palace .....

Near year's end 1989...

Rachel hadn't waited for a final decision from Jim. She knew certain things had to change before he would come to live in this "middle of nowhere" place with her. First of these was her present living condition.

She found a large rent house in town (Fayetteville) and she and the boys moved as soon as it was livable.

The old house had wide doors, wood floors, and two bathrooms (one large enough to maneuver a lift that would be needed for Jim's baths). The house was not air-conditioned but had so many windows that a breeze was almost always moving through.

The entire place was in bad shape but the kitchen was an out and out crime.

A large very stained sink sat beneath a corroded faucet that dripped sulfur water in a steady rhythm. The drips from the blackened spout had made their way into the cracked, ill fitted sink drain and then rotted the floor along the front of the cabinets. The smell of mold mingled with rancid grease set the mood for the rest of the small room.

The cabinet top's once green linoleum covering was warped and winning its battle for freedom. Beyond the cook stove, a decrepit hot water heater wheezed in a small dark pantry. Thankfully, this frightening cubbyhole had a door - making it temporarily forgettable.

An outhouse had more space than the entire kitchen.

Rachel groaned at the added sight of the stove and refrigerator which struggled for position, arguing over whose doors could or could not be opened. The upper cabinets were so high that only the bottom shelf could be reached easily, a stretch reached the second, and the top shelf was beyond all hope of contact without a ladder.

Rachel and Kate surmised that the kitchen had undoubtedly been planned and executed by a male. Executed was a very suitable word.

A doorway on the north side of the godforsaken room, sometimes referred to as the kitchen, opened into a laundry or utility room located on a porch which clung unsteadily to the house. The floor wobbled, creaked, and all surfaces threatened collapse at any moment. Beyond the porch was a large yard, which was completely shaded by tall pecan trees. These had been trimmed at some date long past and a mountain of limbs rotted in the center of the yard. A few rose bushes scattered here and there whispered of by-gone days of splendor.

Doors and windows.........

The house had three very large bedrooms connected by a long L shaped hallway – which turned abruptly behind the living room. There, hunkered down in the shadows, was a huge, rusty kerosene heater, originally intended to aid in heating the house. Each bedroom also contained an open flame propane heater and the giant living room sported a well-smoked fireplace – plus another propane heater. All of these mechanisms to aid in warming the house should have warned of the miserable winter months possible here.

Obviously, at one time, this house had been beautiful and one of the better homes in Fayetteville. The doorways were wide and glass was everywhere. Beveled glass front bookcases lined the walls on either side of the fireplace. Windows lined the south wall of the living room and on the west side, a glass paned double door opened onto the front porch. All of double doors in the house had beveled glass. The porch widened here and produced a large sitting area. One could almost taste the cool lemonade they would enjoy on this pleasant veranda.

Two similar, beveled glass doors opened from the porch here into the room that was to be claimed by Sean (the wizard). One inside door from Sean's room entered Rachel and Jim's room-to-be and another opened into the hallway.

Aaron (the eldest) chose the smallest bedroom located at the end of the hallway on the back side of the house. It had its own bath and shower. This bath was located on the rickety porch and became ... "the boys' bathroom". This bathroom also provided an excellent escape route to the back yard.

Patrick (the youngest - AKA; Bullet or Don Juan Jr.) was given a room near the kitchen. It had been intended as a dining room perhaps, or a study, but with the numerous rooms in the house, this became the fourth bedroom. Patrick's windows looked out into the back yard. Four doors opened into his room. One was to the hallway – near the ugly kerosene heater, another opened into the living room, the third opened into the family room, and the last opened into the kitchen.

The boys could see the advantages of the entire house immediately.

A guy could escape in any direction.

This truly was a house of doors and "windows" – all over standard size. To her dismay, Rachel realized she had to purchase curtains for thirty-one windows, plus curtains for the doors which all had windows as well. A total of eight doors exited the house.

Rachel had a ramp constructed by the east door, which provided wheelchair access to and from the carport.

....

The house was in such bad shape that the landlord in Houston didn't charge anything for the first few months and he didn't ask for a signed lease. It was his way of saying he understood that the house was unlivable as it stood.

And so the monstrous project began. Since white walls were an abomination to Rachel, the house was soon filled with color. All of it was intensely scrubbed and junk that remained inside the house and yard was hauled to an old barn on the back of the property and hidden there. Fayetteville had no facility for such things as old toilet bowls, bathtubs, washers, mattresses and the like. It appeared that other people of the town had been using the old barn for the same thing since the house had been mostly unoccupied for a long time and the building was well stuffed with such refuse.

Unwelcome House Guest.....

The one object Rachel had no notion of what to do with was a very large console piano, which sat stubbornly holding its ground in the family room. This delightful thing emitted wisps of very fragrant mold and possible remnants of a rat's nest somewhere in its entrails. Looking like an old smiling horned owl, it proudly flaunted warped paint, missing keys (the few remaining were of multiple colors), and the sound of it probably disturbed the old masters now in their graves.

The first order given to Rachel's boys in their new home involved this monster and something about *leaving the dead at rest.*

During their tenure in the house, this old piano was moved, against its will, from room to room - ill-suited to any location. A solution was finally found in the smell and appearance of it when someone suggested placing it in the hidden nook on the side porch. It rested there until some later date when the boys and a group of their buddies followed the example of one of the rock groups they had seen destroying their instruments.

They found the destruction of this unwanted house guest totally invigorating. Still, the shell of it remained with its damaged body and face, waiting for some unknown musician to have pity and see its true value.

Chapter Twelve

Time to tell her family.........and the boys...

When Rachel told her mother she and Jim had decided to marry, Kate knew there was no changing her daughter's mind. The two young soul mates had already struggled with the decision and Kate realized that from the moment they fell in love it was too late to save Rachel the pain of his approaching death. The children were another problem now. They did not know Jim very well and if he came into their lives, they would learn to love him and suffer his loss along with their mother.

The conference....

When she could almost see the end of the preparations on the house, Rachel discussed Jim's illness with her sons and asked their feelings about the marriage. She gave them a solemn promise that the final decision rested solely with them and she would abide by it.

The three boys considered the idea in a very serious, private discussion.

Rachel's words....
It was decision time for the boys...December 1989...

Consider the following scenario. Mom sits her three sons down on the couch for an important conference. So important that the television is turned off, something that usually happens only very late at night or during a power failure. She tells them that she loves them more than anything in the world, enough to try to give them a voice in the course the family's life would take. She says that the man in Houston who was her patient has become more than a friend. She loves him. He loves her. They miss each other so much when they are apart it almost hurts, a sad hurt. They want to get married. This would mean he would come to live with them. But he would still be sick, and he would probably die. While he lived it would take a great deal of Mom's time to take care of him, so she wouldn't have as much time with them. They would not be able to go places as much anymore. Money would probably be very tight, she wouldn't be able to buy them toys and clothes like before. They would be able to see their own dad just like before, but yes, this meant that he would not ever be coming back to live with the family. And before the new man died, they might really start to care about him, it would be very hard for them when he was gone. But he wanted to be with them, it would make him happy. It would make Mom happy. If they didn't want her to marry him, she understood, they could always see each other like they had been. She wouldn't be angry or unhappy. She told them that their happiness was the most important thing.

Now, these kids had been around the block. They had been with their mother to her patient's houses before, seen the ventilators and wheelchairs. They had seen her for short little spurts over the last 5 years. She had been a specter that slept while the rest of the world was awake, tried to condense 24 hours of nurturing into four or five chaotic hours of hugs and instructions to the current babysitter in pigeon Spanish or Pilipino, and then disappeared into the night. She had only recently begun to squeeze more time for them in between those long hours that she was gone. Now, she was telling them that she wouldn't have even that much time for them. Money would be tight, less toys from their guilt-ridden mom. Their real dad was irrevocably out of the running in exchange for a man who couldn't play with them, couldn't hold them, and would eventually leave them.

It sounded like a bum deal even as she said it. If someone had offered her a similar proposition she would have questioned their sanity. But she really believed that she could somehow make it right, make all of them happy. So, she asked and then left them alone to decide.

The boys didn't give her a preoccupied yes and return to the Nintendo; or an indignant no, which is what she expected. They really thought it out. They asked her a great many difficult questions and they went away to think some more. Granted, the youngest, at four, was only concerned if the new guy would be playing with his toys, or taking over his bed. However, the two older boys knew exactly what was at stake. At first, they told her that if she didn't mind, they thought they would rather leave things as they were. She said that would be fine, but later, they came back and said that they thought they might want him there after all. They did have one final question: Did Mom think that it really would make him happy to be with them while he could? When she said that she thought so, they told her to tell him, okay.

The oldest boy, Aaron, had been the hold out and she had decided it would have to be all or nothing. He was the closest to his dad, the one who never gave up hope that they would all be together again. He had been old enough to really hurt when his dad left. He knew how bad it could be. He had cried about his own dad and he had cried when he was trying to decide about this new guy. She was astonished when he came to her and asked her to tell him yes.

Rachel

Chapter Thirteen

The House is on Fire

There was always room for more in the Anderson house and somewhere toward the end of 1989 Elyse's husband lost his job. It so happened that their lease was up on their home in San Antonio and so they were invited to come and live on the farm until Andy could reestablish in a new job. This brought them into the time they would all have with Jim.

December 23, 1989...

Christmas was coming and they were preparing for visitors on Christmas Eve. Desserts and all things that could be prepared before the day were ready. On the evening of the 23rd, everyone was tired and so they settled in in the kitchen for an evening of watching TV. Madelyn had not arrived as yet but Rachel, her boys, Elyse and family, plus Keith and Kate were there. The boys spread a large woolen blanket on the floor to keep away the cold. A blast straight from Siberia had hit a few days before and so Keith started a good fire in the wood stove to keep everyone warm. A large propane heater nearby was going full blast as well as the one in the living room, and another on the sun porch but the cold wind was still blowing through the house. It was late, perhaps midnight or so when the family retired. The boys went with their mom, electing to stay in their cottage, and Elyse and family went upstairs to sleep.

Somewhere around one a.m. Keith woke Kate yelling that the house was on fire. Her first sight of it was the blaze going strong where the floor was burning near the wood stove in the kitchen. Somehow, a spark had made its way through the closed grate in the stove. That spark had smoldered for a while there in the blanket and the strong draft had finally fanned the embers into a flame. Within inches of the fire, a huge sheet of plastic had been hung to keep out the cold on the very open east side of the house. Panic was Kate's first response. Keith yelled for her to get water. She quickly filled a dishpan while her husband tried to beat the fire out with a rug or something he had found nearby. She handed him the pan and he yelled again, see about the boys. Both had forgotten that the boys were not there. She started up the kitchen stairs in the heavy smoke and he yelled again....get me more water. She came back down and the process was repeated, i.e. - see about the boys and get me more water. The two of them finally smothered the fire and rushed to check on the family. Thank God, the boys were not there after all. Then she discovered that Elyse and Andy were not in their beds. Kate ran back down the kitchen stairs and as she entered the living room, Elyse, Andy and baby Andrew Gonzales were midway down the west stairwell, staring wide eyed and asking what happened. Kate was unable to answer for laughing at the sight of them. All three had black mustaches, heavy black eyebrows and blackened circles under their eyes. With the heat from the house all going upstairs they had slept beneath a fan - which had coated their faces with much more than ordinary soot from the fire. Their puzzled expressions added to the Kodak moment and Kate, who was half hysterical from the fire anyway, continued to laugh. Keith came in and saved the situation by explaining about the fire. The Poncho Villa trio followed and after making certain that the fire was out, everyone went back to bed.

In the morning, Kate discovered that she and Keith were black from head to toe and their bed was the same. The rest of the house was covered with soot and nothing looked very much like Christmas. Every step across the floor left black footprints, walls and cabinets smeared black with the touch, book's titles were obscured, dishes blackened, curtains shadowed with accents of soot, bed sheets and covers completely blackened, etc. etc.

The first thing she did was call the family they had invited to come and asked them to give them a little more time. A lot of work had to be done but they would still celebrate Christmas Eve as planned. All of that day the family worked frantically, laughed a lot, and felt extremely grateful that an angel (must have been) or something had awakened Keith in time to save them all. Only a few seconds longer and the house would have been an inferno. That went without question.

That evening while opening gifts, they discovered that they had missed some of the fire's remains. There above - to the ceiling... and down through the Christmas tree was a blackened web where a very industrious spider had done her work, making the tree her own. It added a special touch and so the web remained until the tree was taken down. They considered it a reminder of an angel's special gift on that cold December night.

Chapter Fourteen
Running Out of Time

Jim spent a somewhat miserable holiday in Galveston, missing Rachel but they talked often on the phone. Being without her was the final push to convince him that without delay, his happiness was with Rachel and the boys. Their plans locked into place and the wheels began to turn.

Excerpt from Rachel's notes...March of 1990..

We were running out of time. Jim would be moving in with the boys and I on March 1st and only 2 rooms in the entire house were completely painted. My remodeling efforts were as disorganized as everything else I did, and I had been unable to force myself to stick with one project until it was finished. I could give you a preview of the final color or look of almost any room, there were partially painted walls, long strips of wallpaper, partially stained floors throughout the house. And a horde of paint-stiffened brushes. My poor father, who could use the same paintbrush for 20 years through devoted care and cleaning, and who was the soul of organization, had stopped coming by to check on my progress long before. The sight of so much waste and disorder was more than he could bear. As the day that Jim would be moving in drew near, panic took over. The boys and I had moved in in December, with so much of the house unlivable or non-functioning that it was just one step from camping out, but the TV worked, they had their toys, and if we slept in front of the fireplace with enough heavy quilts, we were fairly comfortable, so we had managed. They tend to be excessively messy, and their mother an inept housekeeper, so that the chaos we had moved into was not that unfamiliar

Rachel...

With the deadline nearing, the sisters and Kate stepped in with a vengeance and worked with Rachel to finish the house. They had done what they could in the earlier months but dedication was needed now. Organization helps and when everything was in place the most needed projects surfaced. They worked feverishly to finish the bedrooms and family room. The kitchen was a must and though the smallest room, became the most work. Their palace was still under construction but presentable and all was "ready enough" for Jim to come to his new home at last when the month of March arrived.

Chapter Fifteen

Their Knight in Shining Armor

March was here and Jim was on his way to Fayetteville, Texas, population 268 going on 269.

Their Knight in Shining Armor............

Spring had arrived in south Texas. The old rent house was almost ready - still smelling of fresh paint, wooden floors (waxed to a high gloss), curtains washed, children scrubbed, on the day Jim would see his home and his future in-laws for the first time. Kate and Keith weren't sure exactly what to expect but knew he was disabled and a victim of Lou Gehrig's disease. Regardless of any negatives about him, he was the man their daughter was in love with and was going to marry in very short order.

After a tense morning of anticipation, the New Yorker arrived in the driveway. They watched as Jim Mitchell was lifted from the car and placed in his wheelchair. He appeared fragile and smaller than Kate had imagined. His head popped backward as his family moved up the ramp with him. His red-brown hair was thick and she could see that he had a mustache.

They waited.

Rachel had described his eyes as the most beautiful hazel/blue you have ever seen, and full of life. She was right. Kate's impression of him changed as soon as she looked directly into those eyes and he smiled. Yes, he was a handsome man.

During the early moments of their meeting, Jim wanted Kate to hear some of his music on his CD player. The sound of his favorite *Theme from Somewhere in Time* brought her to tears and included there, portions of variations on *Paganini's Rhapsody* had been her favorite for many years.

They became friends in that instant.

The boys gathered around, laughing and talking. Their knight in shining armor had arrived, a father to live in the house with them. They were excited and if they were hesitant, it didn't show. A real dad to talk to about man things; what a new concept? Mother just couldn't understand the male feelings about all things.

They would soon and often hear Jim say with a sly smile - "that's a guy thing", as though the women could not understand or become involved in a situation. The new stuff coming up with girls was another thing. Mother could help some, being a girl, but guys have certain thoughts on the subject too, and Jim was well schooled on the matter of women. Like Rachel's sons, plus having a military father, he had faced rejection by other boys in towns he had lived in as a boy - having to prove himself in fights and standing up to bullies. He would have good advice there too.

Obviously, the boys were happy at the prospect of becoming a complete family at last, with two parents like most of the other kids in the small Catholic community. Beneath it all was the knowledge that this would be for a short time. Regardless, they would have a dad who loved them, talked to them and answered their questions.

This was a special family and these were very special children.

The Wedding........................

A simple ceremony was planned with the local JP officiating. His wife was invited to come with him. Jim's mother Pat, stepfather

Buddy, his brother Mike and wife Gage, his sister Val, and his grandmother were there. Rachel's family made up the rest of the wedding party - her sister Elyse and husband Andy, their tiny son Andrew, Madelyn - Rachel's youngest sister, and their parents Kate and Keith.

Jim had arrived in Fayetteville a few days earlier and now he was secluded in the back bedroom with his mother, Val and Mike - being dressed in his best suite. The rest of the family chased Rachel about the house, trying to help her prepare for their special moment. Judge Ross examined the marriage license and then all gathered in the living room.

There, in front of the fireplace in the rose room without furniture, a circle of humanity gathered about them and listened as their vows were made.

Kate's most vivid memory of the ceremony was the end when they were pronounced man and wife and Jim began to cry. This was the first time she had seen a groom cry. Because of his illness, Jim sometimes had difficulty hiding his emotions. He was embarrassed by it. Kate thought it was entirely appropriate.

The boys hugged him and their mom, and with a combination of joy and apprehension the witnesses did the same and shared their special moment.

Steaks were cooked on the grill, cake and punch was served and laughter was shared with the newlyweds who only had eyes for one another. Jim's suit was somewhat large for him now, but he looked handsome. Rachel was beaming and beautiful, and the rest of the guests were insignificant bystanders as they watched the new family that day.

One of the main things the family decided to do when they learned he was to be a part of their lives was to never ignore the subject of Jim's illness. They would talk freely about it. This turned out to be a wise decision.

Chapter Sixteen

A whole new world

Jim was thoroughly entertained if not somewhat dismayed at the change from the docile, quiet life he had been living in Galveston with his all-adult family. Anyone would have been amazed, even coming from a household of "standard" kids into Rachel's household and this must have been a real shocker for Jim. Of course, he mistakenly thought he had the quick fix and would straighten out the discipline situation in short order.

Rachel had her hands full before she married Jim, but now she was inundated with requests for every kind of assistance imaginable. A disabled spouse alone is enough to destroy most individuals. The ordinary reaction to continuous care of one adult person who can do nothing for themselves is to place them in a home where someone else can take the strain. Rachel would hear none of it. Jim prodded and pushed her often in the beginning as though testing to see if that would be her ultimate reaction to caring for him.

Meanwhile, the boys pressed to maintain a fair share of her time and Rachel began to disintegrate.

Daddy Jim...

Jim's body was changing but he was still a handsome man. He was full of mischief and loved to banter about everything. He refused to let go of life and believed that he would somehow conquer the disease that was destroying him.

One thing was certain; death was not going to have an easy time of it with this one.

The boys began to call him Daddy Jim.

Three Small Knights.............

Aaron, Sean and Patrick were different than the molded Czechs who lived in Fayetteville. Molded is not meant as mildewed, but the description could be used correctly in some cases. The term is intended as one way, singular of mind, in a rut, and seemingly; void of creative thinking. To Rachel's family, most of the other kids seemed dull. To the residents, the Mitchell crew was eccentric and weird - wild raucous boys out of control - outsiders who didn't belong in their sleepy, reserved, segregated, peaceful sanctuary... and to top it off they weren't even Catholic.

Sean (now age six) and Aaron (age nine) read encyclopedias for entertainment, and all of the boys dressed up as pirates, spacemen, aliens, Ninjas, and all forms of unthinkable beings - wearing colorful scarves, baggy pants, no pants (since Spiderman jockey shorts were appropriate in some cases), men's shirts and sports jackets, and a variety of belts needed to pack weapons made from their mother's curtain rods covered with duct tape. These things were required to enable them to face unseen foes. This attire was appropriate in their way of thinking, to be worn in the local bank, cafés or anywhere about the town square. Ostrich feathers or live frogs didn't matter, since life was full of surprises and so the boys wore them or carried them on their persons.

Aaron's quick temper and Patrick's brought about tremendous fighting between the two- Patrick - the baby of the family (alias Bullet (fleet of foot) or Don Juan - no explanation necessary, and Aaron - the first born (manipulator extraordinaire'). Sean, i.e. Wizard or Wheezer (whose idol was Albert Einstein) was somewhere in between, usually trying to isolate himself from the troublesome twosome. On occasion, they would invade his territory and then the lion was loose.

Sean was usually very busy on his own turf. He had many projects. One involved his civic duty. He began collecting trash about town to be recycled. He decided this was not going to get the job done so he asked for donations at the door of Orsak's Café in an effort to save the world and clean up the environment. He collected almost two dollars from the citizens (who were cautious with every penny) and proudly mailed the money to President Bush (the first). He was crushed when the funds were returned to him with a commendation for his efforts and thanks but no thanks. However a signed letter and an autographed photo of the President brightened things somewhat. Rachel framed the photograph and it went through storms of wild play and the usual deluge that occurs in a room occupied by a boy like Sean.

Sean's nickname as Wizard suited his fascination with potions made from household supplies such as his mother's laundry soap, expensive Chanel perfume, Sean's cologne, Clorox, baking soda, and pepper sauce. He tested these things in various ways. A favorite test was to place the concoction in the microwave. Closed containers, including raw eggs, were lacking information as to their pressure capacity and he decided the microwave could be used for that. Rachel had to be on constant guard for the sound of the microwave. He tested in other ways of course and was disappointed when an entire bottle of his mother's Chanel #5 did not perform adequately as a deodorant for the guinea pig cage.

Rachel's feelings about the matter were somewhat stronger.

Chapter Seventeen

School Days....

The three small knights were like all brothers, fighting one another at a sneeze, but they saw no reason to fight other boys to prove anything. This to them was juvenile. However, boys will be etc. and the local school house contained a number of young roosters spoiling for a fight.

The Fayetteville school building was hidden behind the original, which was an ugly, two story, square, red brick structure. This currently housed the town's museum of Czech culture. The building currently in use for educating the kids of the community was an L shaped facility with an auditorium-cafeteria combined and classrooms looking out into a bland courtyard. The gymnasium, all-purpose portion, was behind the boys' Ag/Shop classroom. The gym was not an expensive model, having only temporary seating. It was not modern but was sufficient for the needs. All grade levels used the cafeteria and gymnasium but the older students were somewhat sequestered adjacent to the front of the complex. This design threw students of all age levels together and this in turn brought much older boys into the battle the new arrivals faced.

In March of 1990, Aaron was completing a second run at the first grade and Sean was completing Kindergarten. Aaron's first grade teacher in Houston had ignored his dyslexia, did not understand ADD, and failed him. It was a terrible blow to a boy who was older than most of his classmates already because his birthday fell in mid-September. He was also very tall for his age and now he was in a new town, still in the first grade, and bigger than the third grade boys.

The bullies couldn't resist a fight with this one.

Being the oldest, Aaron broke ground for the rest. He was the first to reach Fayetteville's front line. He always wanted and needed friends, loved people, and was open and friendly with everyone – the good and the bad. When he entered the Fayetteville school, a select group of the town's boys decided to test Aaron's manhood. A sissy wouldn't be welcome and he had to prove himself. They met after school and told Aaron he had to fight them. He refused. They attacked him and sent him home in tears. A very rumpled boy couldn't understand them hitting him for no reason.

When Rachel rented the house in town, trouble followed Aaron and Sean home from school. Some persons, obviously a platoon of the most devious, slashed the tires of the boys' bikes and broke the lights and reflectors. Toilet tissue draped the trees of their yard more than any house in town, and beer bottles often crashed against the front porch in the middle of the night. Chants and curses were hurled through open windows and cowards ran away into the dark.

A family meeting was called with Grampa, Kate, Rachel, Jim, and the boys in attendance. A long discussion explained, "the way people are". With added courage and the backing of the family, Aaron resolved to change the situation. The problem persisted. He was now the goat, placed there because of the fight that made him cry. This seemed to give the bullies of the school license to tear him apart. He tried valiantly. Following Grampa and Jim's advice, he told the tormentors, "I'll fight one of you, any one of you in a fair fight but I won't fight all of you at one time." The group then fought him one at a time with their own twist – replacements coming in at convenient intervals. He sadly informed the family that the plan didn't work. They had fought him into exhaustion. The PE coach observed all of it but did nothing about it. Aaron knew then that his family was also on the black list in Fayetteville. He learned that grownups are kind now and then, not always fair, sometimes stupid, and often terribly cruel. This included PE teachers.

Nothing seemed to penetrate the mindset of the bullies. The battles continued with Sean and Patrick dragged into the fray – the three standing together against the world, which at this point consisted of the very small clannish town.

Patrick at age four was the most agile of the boys, running like a rabbit and fighting any adversary – provoked or otherwise. One day Rachel looked out the window and saw him chasing an elderly neighbor with a switch. The man had been picking up pecans in Rachel's yard and Patrick was vehemently protecting Mother's territory. He was the third in line and his introduction into the family had brought the usual conflict caused by the third child. The difficulty with his entrance was perhaps more pronounced because of his aggressive behavior and quick temper. To say this one was aggressive and fearless was an understatement.

His parents were going through a post-divorce reconciliation /separation /reconciliation period during this pregnancy. Life was extremely unstable and his mother developed an extraordinary need to protect this tiny child. This understandable need grew into a blind spot that sometimes prevented her from seeing the older boys' side in conflicts with Ryan. This produced the same result as kerosene on a fire. Count those difficulties and add in the fact that Aaron and Sean had already faced far too many rejections and thoughtless neglect from their biological father. These two were very intelligent and understood much more than most boys of their age.

Chapter Eighteen

Attention deficit disorder

To make the recipe for life even more complicated, both of the two older boys were born with attention deficit disorder – a problem their mother shared. She was disorganized and constantly exhausted from trying to be what she could not. The car keys were never on the hook by the door. Her purse was completely missing or its contents scattered. If one entered her living room it was obvious where she had been sitting. The family referred to this area as Rachel's nest. Always late and often accused of being scatterbrained by those who did not understand, her life was lived only in the extreme. Even a simple run to the corner store produced stress because the checkbook could not be found or where was that twenty-dollar bill she had? The clothes she needed were usually in the dryer but had soured because she forgot to turn the dryer on. A multitude of projects were in progress at all times and few tasks were completely finished. Things were nothing short of near chaos in the Mitchell house but with the right spirit, life was also a joyous thing. Laughter was there – more than tears – among the clutter and clatter.

When Rachel was a child, no one had invented the term ADD.

Kate read that such children need structure. They had that in their home. She supposed she was organized in her way of doing things. The only thing she had noticed different about her first born was the fact that Rachel had difficulty sleeping. Kate had trouble keeping her in bed at night. Even as an infant, she usually slept only in fifteen-minute intervals. Being a new mother, Kate thought Rachel had to "sleep like a baby" and she must be doing something wrong. Rachel was extremely curious and Kate lived under a constant barrage of questions from the day she learned to speak. She did not try to teach her daughter her letters or numbers before she started to school. Rachel learned them without Mother. She knew about money, her colors, could count to one hundred and taught herself to read. She was destroyed when her first grade teacher told her that her method of reading was all wrong. Rachel knew what words were because at some point in time mother had told her what the writing said, and Rachel remembered if she saw that word again.

For those who have heard a lot about ADD but don't really understand it, a simple explanation is that those born with this problem cannot focus if any distractions occur. Normally, we can listen to one conversation in a room full of chatter if we choose to do so. A person with ADD cannot possibly do that. If a child with ADD has an earache, he cannot shut out that pain and function normally. I sometimes think of it as trying to sing The National Anthem while a train whistle is blowing in my ear. Life is like that for these children and adults. This is why they prefer the night to daylight, a singular existence to that of a crowd. They cannot keep their minds on any subject for long. A child with ADD will do perhaps three or four problems in Math and become bored to the point that he cannot concentrate to do even one more. Repetition is torture. They are usually very intelligent and if they do not become bored with repetition they can learn extremely fast.

Chapter Nineteen

This was their world

The three boys favored one another in some ways, as most brothers do, but the singular trait they shared was brown eyes like their mom.

Aaron had a quick smile and a spirit to match. His straight blond hair, always bleached to the max by the sun hung in strands down his wide forehead. He was usually sun burned with peeling skin since being outside was his favorite thing. He was also covered with bug bites on his long skinny, knobby kneed legs because insects loved him. He could never leave a bug bite alone and invariably scratched the top off of every one. He said that made it stop itching. This habit caused a trip home from school at the beginning of each school year as the teachers were certain he had the chicken pox. He was willing to try all things new which included cooking and he often served the family meals that would or could never be repeated. His laugh was infectious. He was spoiled by his parents and grandparents as well since he was the first grandchild in Kate and Keith Anderson's family. Clearly

Aaron's greatest gift was manipulation and he practiced that often on his younger brothers. He and Sean were adept at copying dialects and voices and this ability worked exceptionally well during their skits used to entertain the family.

Aaron went about looking for things that he could improve and any way possible to make money. If anyone in the household missed their belt the one to ask about its whereabouts had to be the tall one. He wore as many belts as he could find, each loaded with a gun or weapon of some kind. Brave to the core he was ready for battle at all times.

Sean was a curly haired elf, whose blond curls attracted females young and old. He always cringed when strange women decided they "must" run their fingers through his irresistible hair. He glowered at his brothers during these episodes, daring them to smirk or make any comment whatsoever. He tanned well. That was a blessing because he didn't need sunburn added to his skin problems. He was so allergic to poison oak and its relatives that he often suffered rashes which tried to take over his body. He spoke in a raspy voice due to his asthma and went about humming most of the time. (He obviously sang a lot during school hours as well in that a note was sent home from school stating that he was singing an obscene song during class - a country song with lyrics…"I'm having day dreams about night things in the middle of the afternoon"). Sean's habit of holding his arms folded in front probably came about because he always considered every facet of a situation before making a move. He dressed the opposite of what he should… warm in summer and hardly wore a stitch in winter. There was no explanation for that. One thing was certain, his brain never rested and everyone around him suffered or enjoyed the results. He was like his mother in that he simply did not care for sleeping. He read every printed word that came within his view, collected pamphlets from physicians' offices or the local bank. It did not matter. Things written had to be read. Life was short and he wanted to learn everything possible.

Patrick, who had been the last to enter Rachel's brood was

referred to as "the brat" by his brothers for good reason. He was born with a chip on his shoulder and no one had dared knock it off. He was somewhat like a rat terrier who would attack a Doberman. He had no awareness of his size. Being the youngest, smallest brother meant nothing to him. What he did know was that no one could catch him if he decided he needed to leave for some reason and if he decided to stand and fight it didn't matter a wit if he won the fight or not. The other guy was going to regret that he started anything with him. He was also tagged the pretty boy, always overly particular about his clothes. His ash brown hair had to be cut just so. Kate hated cutting it because the procedure seemed endless as she tried to please the little prince.

Allergies plagued all of the boys and the medicine cabinet was filled with an array of remedies that only seemed to raise their level of hyperactivity. Aaron…the string bean kid, all arms, legs, and big feet could never catch Patrick in a chase. The same was true of Sean, who was solid and not so stringy. He ran with a gait that caused him to be called crazy legs, Patrick was still young enough that he had little flesh on his bones but all three were taller than their friends of the same age. Jim surmised that they would grow to six feet or more.

He was right on the money without ever knowing.

All of the boys were adept at making any number of strange and complicated things from Legos or any object they could pry loose from anywhere in the house. The flatware disappeared with regularity, as did the faucets…yes, faucets…those with cutoffs whose mechanisms Sean had figured out, curtain rods, and even the bars that held the clothes in the closets.…these made good jousting rods, shepherds staffs and such…The removal of the curtain and closet rods caused Rachel much despair. She was continually having to iron curtains that had been summarily dumped on the floor or clothing that forever lay in crumpled heaps in the closets. The ironing board in Rachel's house stood at the ready day and night. It was never retired or put away for a single day. Kate hated it and told Rachel that one day they were going to have a ceremony and burn the thing in the front yard. That possibility was something to look forward to anyway.

Kate and Rachel made regular tours of the yard, retrieving silverware and kitchen utensils. Hammers, screwdrivers, wrenches, any tools that Rachel owned which were never in the tool box. Every project first required an APB search for those things needed to accomplish it. Keith found this disregard for tools an absolute outrage. He and Rachel had fought during all of her years at home over the subject of his tools. This continued to a point that Rachel once wrote a last will and testament to her father and left all of her tools to him as an offer of settlement for past debts.

One of the tools that could usually be located at Rachel's was the pliers. They were most likely in the bathroom, their presence required there because of the continually missing handles to the faucets. Kate could think of no use for a faucet other than its intended purpose but obviously someone in the household thought otherwise.

Sean loved books more than the other boys and probably because of his extensive reading, understood game instructions easily. He explained the rules of board games, cards and the like to his brothers, though they tried his patience. He seemed to be able to understand anything he read at one sitting and became frustrated when Aaron and Patrick would not put forth the effort to learn the rules. Actually, Aaron didn't care that much about rules. He preferred his own anyway and intense arguments were a part of most games.

When they played Chess, Sean always won the first game. His concentration could last only so long and his brothers soon learned that they could beat this impatient soul if they could force him to play a second game. He usually reluctantly succumbed to their taunts and lost the second round.

Jim enjoyed watching their exchanges. He refereed when required and joined their games whenever possible.

Patrick's steady hand......

Patrick loved to wrestle with his new dad, positioning himself close enough for Jim to grab him with his feet while struggling violently to get away. Sometimes, he rode on Jim's lap in the wheelchair, squealing with delight as though they were on a Harley, racing about the house. Patrick had a very steady hand and began shaving Jim. He was only four years old but he was very cautious and able to do an excellent job of it.

Trust came easily to Jim and love came easily to all of them.

With Aaron, many hours were spent watching Star Trek and discussing space travel. Jim wanted to go and thought Aaron would have the opportunity someday. Aaron bounced his ideas for inventions off of Jim and these were continuous. Aaron's mind was always racing, solving the world's problems through technology. Controlling, sweet, kind, boisterous combative, angry, gentle and full of laughter - that was Aaron. He loved to cook, sometimes wonderful things, sometimes questionable dishes, but who argues with the chef when no-one else wants to cook?

As with most households, absolutely no-one wanted to wash the dirty dishes and Aaron-the-Chef usually left a profound mess in the kitchen. He was inventive in that way too. The kitchen could have easily forgotten what it was supposed to be by the time Aaron finished his cooking projects.

As seems to be the custom in a house full of males, the dirty jobs were always left to Mother. If Kate found the kitchen piled high, she usually threatened an act of congress in order to force the boys hand with the dishes. With that threat, she shouldn't have been surprised when that choice of discipline worked about as well as most acts of Congress do.

She marveled at the layers of mess Aaron-the-Chef could produce during his culinary efforts. Flour was always (piled) on the stovetop and floors in abundance, grease was splattered from the heat being much too high and the amount of dishes and pots dirtied in the process was simply amazing. It seemed that he had solved the problem of scant cabinet top space by special construction. Clearing that was like playing the game of Pick Up Sticks. You had to make sure you removed the dish that would not send the rest to oblivion and there was no room left in the sink for one more thing.

However, the boys said the food was delicious if perhaps a bit spicy.

One kitchen mess that was standard and constant was a large splattering of coffee grounds from the boys preparing their mom's coffee, a ritual that was duplicated many times throughout each day.

....

Sean, who only worked alone on his projects, seldom cooked and he spent a lot of time with Jim.

A bond grew between a man in a wheelchair and another man in a boy's body. The absent minded professor, this middle child was soft hearted and gentle, always kind to Jim though often obstinate with his brothers. He and Jim had long question and answer sessions with Sean probing Jim's mind for answers to questions about everything Jim knew and that was a great deal. Jim devised games and puzzles on his computer to test Sean when he came home from school and watched proudly as Sean absorbed everything. If he had difficulty Jim was there with the answer.

Jim was there for all of the family in that way. He was helpless in that chair but he took everyone through the steps of repairing things about the house - using their hands.

Rachel believed in allowing her boys *freedom to be themselves.* They took full advantage of that mindset with overwhelming results. Still, all was not negative. The boys were extreme clowns. Ideas bounced around that house like fireworks and surprises were constant.

Kate often found the boys frustrating in their inability to concentrate, forgetting what they were supposed to do the moment they walked out of the room. They became frustrated at themselves. They wanted to succeed more than anyone.

Rachel and her mom were invited more than once to visit the teachers at the school. The most memorable object of these visits was the sight of the boys' desks, stuffed full and running over with unfinished work. It was a symptom of their ADD, this inability to complete any project. Regardless of their paperwork difficulties, they learned.

Their reaction to scolding was like their concentration about other things. They quickly forgot every word.

Jokes came easily to Aaron and Sean. They performed their comic routines continuously, leaving all of the family exhausted with laughter from all of the disjointed conversations and distractions. Both boys kept up with the world and local news like adults and collected a wide variety of ideas for their skits. Early on they developed the ability to mimic dialects and personalities. They also tried their hand at learning guitar and learned well enough but were usually too busy with other things to concentrate on that for long periods. As far as special musical talents, they occasionally performed a duet (or trio when they could convince Patrick to join them) by making their ears squeak in unison. They said it was Jingle Bells they were playing, or something of the sort.

Chapter Twenty

A family project

The fun and mayhem continued and Jim became the next family project.

Rachel and Kate had decided that since the doctors had given up on helping Jim, the family would have to find a way to do something for him themselves.

When Keith became ill back in 1978, Kate collected books and searched the public libraries for information about the human body's healing abilities. She learned that nutrition was a key ignored by most physicians. In her efforts to ward off the disease affecting Keith's kidneys, she had succeeded to some degree because his kidneys had lasted five years rather than the two predicted by his doctors. Using her books once more, she contacted a rep of Wachter products. They sold supplements made from sea plants and in Kate's opinion these held the best hope for Jim.

Rachel ordered a supply of the strongest green powders Watcher's sold, purchased a juicer to make the best of all juices, although not the most delicious drinks, for Jim. While he could swallow, he dutifully drank these awful solutions. Not only was Jim not giving up, the family wasn't giving up either.

As they had planned, they talked openly about the subject of Jim's illness any time it came up. The method helped to sidestep the pain involved, talking it out, as though the discussion was of a bill they were unable to pay or last night's mealtime leftovers. They cried with him, for him and themselves, and then they laughed together about some nonsense.

Life seemed normal even though it was not.

Chapter Twenty One

Jim's first summer in Fayetteville

It was a hot, very busy summer with the extended family coming and going with regularity at the farm, and the boys forever keeping Jim well entertained.

Rachel, Jim and the boys spent the newly formed Mitchell family's first Fourth of July with the Andersons, including Madelyn and a few of her multitude of friends.

The rains came in the summer of 1990 and fire wasn't a fear so Keith agreed to a celebration on the tennis court. It provided space for a barbecue and everyone, particularly Jim, wouldn't be in danger of the fire ants getting to them. Madelyn brought a lot of fireworks and with those added by everyone a great show was enjoyed by all.

As far as the farm animals it was fun even before the fireworks began and they took part in the festivities with the roosters chasing the boys as they often did. The gander did his part strutting around honking and attacking when anyone there turned their back on him. All of their antics added to the eventful celebration.

Jim loved coming out to the farm watching the animals. On

one such occasion the pigs got out of their pen, again. Pigs are intelligent and the fences in the corral and pig pen were not too dependable. Kate often heard the squeal from the boys "the pigs are out" and so each time a mad chase was on. Communicating with pigs is no small thing and yelling seemed to be of no value. The pigs usually talked only to one another about which direction would be the best one to find freedom and didn't give up too easily. Everyone grabbed sticks and when they weren't all laughing too hard, they worked together to move the duo that had no desire to go back into that boring pig pen. You couldn't head them off at the pass with all of that open space. Kate's broom took a beating as she worked to head the pigs in the direction of the barn. A few runs around Jim's wheelchair brought him into the middle of the fray but his tactic was to simply try to be invisible to the pigs.

Along with the pigs, the geese tried to add to the entertainment by exhibiting the stupidity of the gander. The goose was very intelligent and usually had to show the gander where the feed was etc. On one occasion, Jim and the family watched as she went through a hole in the fence and headed down the hill. The gander became desperate immediately and began honking and calling her back. A two way honking session began. She patiently waddled back to the fence and tried to console him but he was so frantic he would hardly listen. At last he calmed down and she stuck her head back through the large hole in the fence, indicating that *this* was the place he could step through. Somehow, he missed the point and began running back and forth along the fence. She caught up with him on the other side and led him back to the hole. The family watched as she patiently tried again and again to show him where he could reach her by poking her head back and forth through that large hole. After a long session, she gave up and came back through the fence. They waddled off together, the gander strutting with his head high as though he had done a marvelous thing.

Back at the Mitchell house in town...........

The oldest boy in the household was Jim….

Jim was still a boy, much like his new sons, interested in all of life, learning and observing as though he would someday have the tomorrows to use the knowledge. He tugged at a soft place in all of the family when he would say "when I get well I will do this or that." They wanted to believe it could be so and Jim was so positive about this self-founded fact that they sometimes did, making plans together for that distant event, the day he would teach the boys karate, basketball, football, scuba diving, astronomy, or cook for the family.

During fast moving conversations, Jim worked furiously, making his light talker interject "what she said, what he said." He added his own flavor by changing the voice tones on the talker. One of the favorite things everyone loved to do with Jim was to suggest the letters he might use together to produce the raspberry and other such expressive sounds that might be useful to him. Use your own imagination as to the things the boys thought he might use. They were never successful with the raspberry but the sounds produced by the ideas thrown in were more than interesting. He had key phrases at the ready and when he hit the wrong button, the game would begin again and the family was off the track, laughing and inventing other bizarre noises with a lot of ph, th, zththyd, jkkjbjmzr etc. combinations. He made the light talker sing, sounding somewhat like George Jones, Dean Martin, Frank Sinatra, or Tammy Wynette - which was a family favorite.

Jim often said each new day and night held surprises of some sort usually provided by his new sons. At night, he didn't mind the boys' noises so much but just beyond the back hedge row of the house, a cow pasture complete with hungry mooing cows bothered him. The other thing was a little Bantam rooster someone had given Rachel and the boys. The bird would not hang around. No one ever saw him during the day, but he did not forget his duty and before daylight every morning, he came and stood beneath Jim & Rachel's bedroom window and told them loud and clear, that it was time to get up. Jim was saddened when the little guy quit coming. Obviously, he was unable to for some unchangeable reason. Hopefully, he had not become someone's dinner.

All were welcome …..

Rachel had always been a champion of the down trodden and this did not change in Fayetteville.…If anyone, or any animal came to her door, they were welcomed. One of these guests was a very old dog who came by for a short visit and couldn't stay away after that. Her name was Star.

Star's yard décor………….

Star was a large unloved, black, collie mix, town dog. Someone owned her but she was a free spirit and went where she pleased, mostly she pleased being at the Mitchells. She had chunks of hair falling off winter and summer and smelled loud enough to keep most people at a good distance. Somehow she had managed to become acquainted with the boys and Rachel and selected them as her favorite family. The affection she received at Rachel's was returned with gifts Star found in her travels. She brought shoes, articles of clothing, bones, and fish heads. One such gift was quite large. Kate was startled when she drove into the driveway and saw an entire cow's leg standing on end in the center of the front yard. It looked as if the rest of the animal might be attached and hidden underground. The boys liked the decoration, and so it remained for a few days to please them and the old dog.

Star continued as an extended member of the family until the boys discovered her beneath their house. She had decided that this home she loved would be the place she breathed her last, and so it was.

Baby mice……

The Mitchell House as their home became known, was filled with pets. Everything living was welcome. Jim hated fleas, spiders, flies and the giant land roaches but all else were permitted. On one occasion, the boys captured some baby mice. Kate had to do some fast talking there. The boys finally agreed to allow her to take them to a pasture far from any farm house and set them free. She did this, feeling rather foolish, and even hoped that the mice might survive the hawks and other predators because of the trust Rachel's boys had placed in her.

This love of almost all of God's creations was a thing Kate had always had to deal with with Rachel. As a child, this daughter had stopped speaking to her father for a week because he ran over a frog in the driveway. On another occasion, she decided her little sister, Elyse was the most evil person alive because she found her pulling the wings off of flies and watching them swim around in circles in the commode.

Skunk......

An open field was beyond the barn in the Mitchell's back yard. A skunk who lived there wandered in, now and then, to examine the garbage cans during the night. Rachel refused to call animal control because the skunk had a right to be there the same as anyone else.

Besides, the overwhelming stench of him didn't wake the family. They seldom went to bed anyway.

A ring necked parrot named Charlie........

The first pet the boys had taken with them in the move to town was a ring necked parrot named Charlie. He was a rather vindictive little bird because he had had a near death experience with Patrick. He discovered that you do not take a bite out of Patrick even when he deserves it. The day he did that, Kate found Charlie quivering with feet up in the bottom of his cage. He was soaked with wasp spray, which was the first weapon Patrick saw when he needed it. Kate grabbed the luckless bird and soused him in sudsy dishwater. She scrubbed him and removed all of the poison. Afterwards, he sat disgruntled and angry with feathers askew, not feeling well at all for several days. He took aim at the boys toys after that and at every opportunity, he thoroughly chewed every action figure he could get his beak on.

Jim developed a special relationship with this family pet. His methods were different than Patrick's since his physical abilities were limited. He sometimes tried to control Charlie by staring at him. Oddly enough, that worked - now and then. Charlie's main purpose toward his new master seemed to be to dismantle everything electronic in the house. He must have noted that Jim used all of those "wired things" a great deal. Charlie's beak was a handy instrument and he used it continually. That bird was smart and knew exactly how to harass Jim. He quickly learned that certain things were off limits to him and of course, those certain things quickly became Charlie's very favorite. In this process or war between these two males, Charlie severed the cord of Jim's stereo and chewed the buttons off of his remote that he kept at his feet. This produced the usual chase between Jim and the bird, one waddling in bird fashion, one crab walking in the wheel chair … going round and round through the house. Jim had to move backward in the chair as he still had enough strength in his legs to push himself about looking somewhat like a crab on the beach.

The confrontations with Charlie always ended with laughter and the boys involved in the chase with the bird squawking, using all of the foul fowl language he could manage.

Kate usually insisted that Jim could easily solve the problem of Charlie by simply leaving him in his cage. In his moment of disgust with the bird, Jim always agreed and watched intently as Kate wired the door and all other possible escape portals to the cage shut while lecturing the boys to "leave things alone."…things meaning the entire cage. Without fail, Charlie would be on the loose the next time Kate visited. Jim feigned innocence but it was obvious that "he who observed everything" was the one who had instructed the boys or Rachel to release the troublesome feathered beast.

Jim could not bear to see anything caged, not even troublesome Charlie.

Chapter Twenty Two
His Beautiful Rachel

Jim would have loved to give rather than receive as his illness had forced him to do. He talked about it often. He wanted to be able to wake his Rachel with a fresh cup of coffee in the morning and give her breakfast in bed. He wanted to pamper and care for her. It would have given him tremendous pleasure. When she left her mother and husband alone in the room, he usually spoke of his love for Rachel and how beautiful she was. She would return to the room with paint splotched clothes, strawberry blond hair in limp strings about her tired face, and dark circles beneath her eyes, exhausted from the hours of care required for Jim and her three sons. He saw her more clearly than any man ever had before. He was right. She was truly beautiful.

Chapter Twenty Three

To The Rescue

When the nursing care stopped somewhere about April, it was automatic for the family to adjust quickly to the new disaster. This time, Elyse being there helped tremendously since she volunteered to stay with Jim so Rachel could continue working and things worked out well for a while. Elyse had an opportunity to become better acquainted with Jim and they became good friends. She was bright and had a lot of knowledge about trivia and things not so trivial and Jim enjoyed talking with her.

He could still swallow food at that point of his illness and so she cooked for him, things he wanted such as scrambled eggs with garlic and butter. He loved extra spices on everything. Since he could not use his hands, Elyse had to spoon feed him. He had difficulty swallowing and usually ate very little. The most tiring thing for her was the fact that Jim was a night owl like Rachel. He wanted to have someone to talk to and Elyse was the least talkative of all of the

Andersons. He questioned her about Rachel, wanting to know everything about her childhood.

The boys and Jim were constant care. The kids wouldn't sleep, made messes, wanted food, needed refereeing, and missed their mom. Elyse couldn't go to sleep at night before Jim, since he had to have help getting out of his wheelchair and into bed. Still, she continued for five months loving and caring for her sister and Jim and the boys.

Elyse went home to the farm and her son Andrew during the day. Andrew was a beautiful little boy, dark and handsome, bright eyed and always laughing. He became famous in the family for being able to call the cows in from the pasture and was very adept at stealing candy from the shelf in Grandma's pantry. He was still a toddler but well able to keep up with his cousins at the Mitchell house. Elyse and Kate spent a great deal of time there helping out and so the three became four busy boys.

Andrew joined his cousins in their wild garb and boisterous games about the house. Elyse often worried that he was learning way too much in that house.

Two distressing moments happened during those visits, only two being something of a record. The first involved an open can of varnish Andrew discovered in Rachel's bathroom. He found the unique solution interesting and played in it with almost disastrous results. As babies will do, his final test was to taste the mixture. He screamed at the burning, overpowering taste and Kate and Elyse quickly cleaned his mouth and hands. Kate also soothed a very frightened mother.

The second distressing moment came when little Andrew decided he was tired of being there.

The number of exits from the Mitchell house was a terror to a young mother. The older boys were given instructions to keep an eye out for their little cousin while the women worked and everyone was trying to be diligent in following that directive. Regardless, somewhere about mid-morning, Elyse began running through the house calling her baby. No response quickly aroused the house and the hunt was on. Desperation was overcoming Elyse when she looked down the street in front of the house. There was little Andrew, happily on his way to the town square on his own private safari.

After that day, assignments to watch Andrew were specific rather than general.

Jim and Keith and Andy and the Dallas Cowboys....

Jim enjoyed being with Andy and Keith. They had many hours of talking and watching the Dallas Cowboys. Jim enjoyed the sessions and beamed with pleasure as they spent this time together. This was an opportunity for man talk and all that means to the male gender. The entire family would eventually join in, talking for hours. These were much more than casual family gatherings for Jim. Rachel said he talked about these sessions for days afterwards.

Chapter Twenty Four

Green drink

Meanwhile, Jim continued to faithfully drink the green concoction Rachel gave him. One happy day, Kate arrived at the house and Jim had a surprise. He called her into the family room and demonstrated his new ability to raise his arms about six inches. The family was elated but now a new problem developed. Jim was losing weight and swallowing was becoming almost impossible.

It was time for a feeding tube.

Near tragedy with the surgery...

Rachel insisted on being in the room when Jim's surgery was performed to place the feeding tube. She watched intently and in the midst of the procedure she noticed Jim's face was blue. He was choking and unable to breath. She sounded the alarm and soon they were working over Jim.

Feeding tube is much too small...

When they arrived home from the hospital, Rachel tried to feed

Jim his special concoction but the tube was too small. Nothing but Ensure and water would go through it. He was losing his ability to swallow even his own saliva and he could no longer receive the healing drink. They were afraid to have another tube placed after his near death with the first one. The incident in surgery had frightened Jim and so the insufficient tube remained.

Laughter and sorrow remained side by side in their daily lives.

This was their world. The family could not cure Jim's ALS and they could not cure the kids ADD, so they made the best of it.

In dealing with the boys, Kate could understand Rachel's light-handed discipline. It was more than difficult to remain neutral when a stern approach was called for, and extremely tiring. People who knew nothing about the realities of ADD always thought they had the method that would resolve the problem.

They were wrong.

Those who have not lived with a true ADD child simply do not, cannot, have a clue. With the confidence of experience, everyone can be included in that group, even the experts.

Kate thought they were possibly the messiest kids ever born. They could never remember to replace the lid on the peanut butter, close the cabinet doors, and sometimes even the refrigerator. Clutter followed them wherever they went like a cloud of dust in a whirlwind.

Sleepless nights.........

Kate lost hours of sleep following Rachel's marriage to Jim. Her mind was filled with fear for the days and years ahead for a dear little gaggle of boys and two young parents who were obviously so deeply in love.

The truth of it was something that could not be changed but Kate questioned the God she believed in about his reasons. Maybe it was for Jim and maybe it was for the Anderson family. Life seemed filled with lessons. Kate surmised that this one was about love.

Everyone has lessons to learn. Kate found comfort in her faith but also guilt. Perhaps there was something she was supposed to do. She had been told that answers always come over time.

When they came to her at last, they fell upon her in a rush of pain and understanding she had not expected.

Chapter Twenty Five

Daily Life

Jim didn't use his light talker all of the time. His speech was slurred and many people had difficulty understanding him. For some reason, Kate did not. Often he was uncomfortable with the depth of her understanding and penetration of his thoughts. He tried to hide his pain and when she saw it, he became vulnerable, unable to pretend he had everything under control.

He had been married before but explained that he had not had a mother-in-law in that marriage and didn't know exactly what to expect from this one. As time passed, he became completely at ease in their discussions. His love for debating became obvious early on and the arguing with Kate seemed to give him a feeling of self-worth. Having a father with the same love for bantering, Kate was able to hold her own and the two developed a habit of playfully telling the other "you're wrong" at the end of each visit.

Kate went to visit the little family often, checking on their needs and trying to help out. Rachel needed someone to help her focus and complete her work. Kate folded clothes and reminded her to push the button on the washing machine that was always full. Rachel usually had a dozen or so unfinished projects going.

The boys were in the same operating mode as their mom and so they became a huge part of the focusing. Kate had been a force to reckon with as far as the little guys were concerned because she was relentless in reminding them to complete tasks about the house. Rachel, forgetful like her sons, could never remember to remind them. Rachel found an old German helmet from WWII at an antique store. The boys wanted to buy it for Kate. It seemed appropriate to them since they called her the General. The helmet became another part of work days since Kate wore it on occasion. Somehow it made following her commands more fun.

They had many catch up days, even with Kate bird-dogging the boys. It usually took at least half of the day to get them moving. She compared it to rounding up a room full of ping pong balls during an earthquake.

During those work days, Jim needed occasional haircuts and Kate enjoyed doing that for him. This prevented prying eyes from disturbing his privacy as they would in a public barber shop. If he was displeased by the results he never said so.

On one such work day, the heat was particularly intense. Kate had been standing on her head for the most part, picking up clutter, toys, books, whatever...left by the boys. Rachel came into the room with Jim and observed her mother for a while before going and gathering the boys. She lined them up in front of a very busy Kate, whose face was red as a turkey gobbler, hair frizzed to the max and perspiration pouring. Rachel told the boys to stand at attention in front of Kate. With a lot of foot shuffling etc. things finally quieted down and Rachel said, "Now, do you boys see what you've done to your Grandmother?" The lesson was not taken as Rachel had intended. The boys found Kate's appearance hilarious and soon Jim and Rachel joined in. Kate went to a mirror and began laughing as well. The only thing that would have made it better would have been the German helmet.

Chapter Twenty Six
Facing the inevitable

As with everyone, Jim could be many people, but the illness was peeling him down to the core of his being. He sometimes talked of his concern about the moment when death came and how he would face it. Then, he would change and say, I've been ready for it for a long time now. I've faced it and that's behind me. Following those words, he would look at Kate with eyes uncertain and question her about her faith in God. Was he real and how did she know?

As the months flashed by, they had many long talks about courage and truth, possibilities and hopes.

Do you believe in UFOs...?

Kate was born into a family with a profound faith in God. It was a natural thing to believe - a part of who she was. Jim had a more skeptical upbringing. His mother was a Chemistry teacher, schooled in scientific thinking. In facing his illness and its prognosis, Jim had studied the Bible and searched for a faith that eluded him. He was proud to think of himself as being scientific minded like his mother. In one of the in-law question and answer sessions, he asked once more why Kate believed. She decided to share with him a special moment that until that day had been shared with very few.

The basis for this strange happening was the fact that Kate had once lost her faith for a period of almost thirteen years. The reason for that loss is insignificant here. What was, was that her struggle had been similar to the one Jim was having. She wondered as she talked with him that day if perhaps God's plan had been that she was to have that earlier experience in order to be able to help this young man in this hour. She had been taught that God reassures only those he chooses and perhaps who have to have that reassurance to believe. Kate had returned to God when the incident in Houston happened but her faith was still weak and questioning. She knew, whatever her problems were, she should relate her experience to Jim.

The moment was strange and unexpected.

Kate knew she was no different than any other living soul. She was far from a saint and definitely no more deserving of anything from a divine spirit than the next person - but something happened that made her wonder if she had been visited by a messenger from God. She had prayed many times for a sign that He was real over the span of those thirteen years and He had not answered. She had been left to muddle her way through, studying and looking and listening for God like a deaf bat.

All of her life, she had said the same short prayer each day. It was a little habit she had. In the early days of her marriage to Keith, while her four daughters were small. Sometimes she said the little prayer many times throughout her day. It was simple..."Lord walk with me." She never really expected an answer to that one. She simply wanted to welcome Him to be present there in her home, helping her cope with many things.

As was her custom, on the day of the happening, she walked across the street from one office of the Texas Research Institute of Mental Sciences to another. She stopped for a moment and sat down on a cement block. She collected her papers and listened to the noise of the city. Then, as she got up to go back to her office, she said her usual prayer. "Lord Walk with me."

At that moment, an entity she could not see, came and stood beside her. She saw nothing, only felt his presence. He surrounded her with a veil of love that she could never describe. It was a love she had never felt before. It overwhelmed her, completely absorbing all that she was. He walked beside her then, through the hedge row, onto the sidewalk and toward the traffic light on the corner. The cars still raced by on the street, people walked past her (unaware) and he remained. She spoke to him with her mind. He did not answer, only comforted her as they walked together in a kind of invisible cocoon. She repeated over and again, "you are here, you are really here." She thought her heart would burst. She was happier than she had ever been, drenched in that beautiful love.

Suddenly, when she reached the corner and stood there with him among the crowd of people, she felt a pang of guilt at having asked him to come. Others must need him much more than she. She said to him, "I am alright now." The words were no sooner out of her mind than she physically felt him leave her. It began at her feet and moved up her body... up and away - above and gone like a cloud that was there but was not. She wanted to take back her words and remain in that pool of love, but it was too late.

She felt numb and alone and confused about what had just happened to her, or had it? Was her mind playing tricks on her?

The light changed and she moved on across the street with the other pedestrians. Immediately she began to ask herself if it really happened to her and why. She tried many times to bring the entity back but the feeling or person never returned in that way again.

When she shared this with Jim, she asked him if he believed her. He said, "I believe you believe it happened."

She then asked him to consider this. She told him "Jim, suppose I saw a red pickup truck go past me in the street. It raced around a corner and out of sight. Other people then came and stood beside me. A policeman drove up and asked if we had seen a red pickup truck. I said I did, but the others said they did not. Now, I ask you, could I prove to anyone there that I saw that truck? No. But, does that mean that I did not see it, that it was not there? Think about it. Just because it is one man's truth only, does not mean that it is not the pure and unchangeable truth."

He grinned and asked, "Do you believe in UFOs?"

Ignoring this skepticism, she answered and said, "There might be such a thing. I've never seen one but that doesn't mean that other people haven't. I'm certainly not going to be fool enough to argue with something I know nothing about. When it becomes important for me to make a decision about UFOs, I will."

He seemed pleased with her answer and they talked longer about God and His love for Jim. He wanted to believe but didn't want to run to God only to flee from his illness and its outcome. He wanted to go to God because he believed.

Kate said, "I've always been told by those with a strong, unshakable faith that the heart of God is waiting for you to come. If He is who the faithful say He is, then we are all the most fortunate spirits possible. Sometimes, I think we who are strong willed have the most difficult time believing. We want to be brave and face everything that comes on our own. Still, I wonder why we are so stubborn that we cannot accept such a beautiful gift as one that is based on love and only love."

In answering Jim, Kate learned things about herself and so they helped one another.

Rachel came to Kate after that particular talk she had with Jim and said he was disturbed because Kate had gotten inside his head. He said, no-one else had ever been able to do that."

Chapter Twenty Seven

Histamine

Jim always tried to not ask for assistance and the family had to be aware of his discomfort. His eyes would water or he would move his face, trying to resolve a nose that itched or the pain caused by histamine in his eyes. Something about his illness caused a heavy secretion of histamine from his skin. If anyone touched him and then rubbed their own eyes they would feel the sting.

The family watched him closely and protected him in every way possible.

When Rachel began taking care of Jim she told Kate about the skin rashes he suffered. When she explained about the oil on his skin that burned, Kate suggested cleaning his skin with Isopropyl Alcohol to dry up the oil. This was not recommended by the physicians and the nursing service objected when Rachel tried it. Jim wanted to continue the treatment. It was the only thing that worked. The oil clogged the pores of his skin and then formed a crust on the surface. The rash followed and so the apparent dryness of the flaking skin made the physicians believe that alcohol would only dry it further. The opposite was true and his skin improved considerably with Rachel's alcohol sponges and only small patches appeared for short periods.

Chapter Twenty Eight

Lost strongholds

We have many plateaus in our lives. Sometimes we are aware of them. In a terminal illness those plateaus are vivid and always there, one more step in a long struggle. The family watched as Jim made his way down each slope, and tried to maintain his foothold, his composure - being ordinary when the turmoil inside was pulling him down. He did not want anyone to suffer because of him. Somehow, this was his fault, this illness. He was the one chosen to have it, therefore, he had to keep it to himself or it was some kind of a crime.

Guilt seems to sit on the shoulder of those who cannot control their circumstance. Common sense says it is a foolish notion, but the heart feels otherwise.

When people are in deep depression or extremely happy, some believe that an aura of color forms about them. With Jim, Kate could see when depression had control. She didn't have to see his face or hear his voice to know. It was as if something, almost a shadow surrounded him. Each time, the sight tugged at her heart and made her hold her breath as she tried to add nothing to his struggle.

Rachel's words regarding Jim's battle.....

Jim was given many gifts at birth, I am certain, and the one proving most useful to him now is his will power. His physical strength gone, he seems to be clinging to life with such a determined will that each step down brings a struggle that all of us in the family can feel. His mind gives way to anger as he denies the count that has once again gone against him, then he lifts himself up to the top of the pit where he has fallen and makes his stand once more........   Rachel

Chapter Twenty Nine

The parade ... 1990

Fayetteville had a unique little celebration each year that they called Lick Skillet. They said it came about because of some past gathering in which they ran out of food for the celebration and licked the skillet clean. The first year of his marriage to Rachel, Jim attended the Lick Skillet parade.

All of the family thought it was delightful.

Sean and Aaron were in that parade. Sean rode on a float with all of his kindergarten classmates, all dressed as clowns. Rachel admonished Sean as the float passed to "put your nose back on". He wore a curly multicolored wig which would have been unnecessary if she had died his curly hair in those odd colors. Another float featured an old outhouse with a hillbilly standing beside it holding a shotgun. The outhouse appeared to be occupied. A moonshine still was perched above smoldering coals in the center of the float and a dejected, defeated revenuer was tied to a nearby tree stump. The shotgun was fired by the hillbilly at intervals with a loud blast causing squeals from the ladies and children nearby. Another hilarious float was displayed by a group of young backwoods hunters riding in an old crinkled convertible which was covered with cattails. Beer cans and hound dogs trailed behind clattering and baying at the crowd (in that order). A stuffed goose flew awkwardly out front of the car with the assistance of a fishing pole support. Behind this spectacle an innocent group of boy scouts with Aaron in the forefront marched with their banner held askew but mostly unnoticed above the smiles of the boys in their new uniforms. Little girls in pretty dresses rode in toy cars and small boys rode bikes wrapped in crepe paper. The town fire truck carried the senior class, whose members threw candy to the crowd and the local oompha band delighted the crowd from the back of a flatbed hay wagon as they played polkas and made the people dance.

Jim loved it and the delight of it was that the parade was so short that it circled the square twice, doubling the fun.

Kolaches (all kinds), barbecue, and numerous desserts were served along with popcorn and other treats. Then, a walk of two short blocks and the family was home again with full bellies and high spirits.

Lick skillet, 1991

When the second September came, Jim's illness had progressed to the point that he was not physically up to going to the Lick skillet parade. At that point, people stared at him so incessantly that he felt awkward in public and also, tired so easily that he could not face going to the little parade on the square with the family.

They were all laughing, yelling "put on your shoes" and getting ready to go. Jim was sitting by his computer, staring at it and saying little. Kate took his hand and said, "Jim, I want you to know something. We are all going on, going off and leaving you, but we aren't really leaving you. You have to know that even though we are going on with things as though nothing is happening, we are aware, completely aware of you and your feelings. We want you with us. I just didn't want you to feel as if we are going on our merry way, leaving you here and being thoughtless. We love you, you know. We care."

He looked at her and raised his eyebrows. Tears came into his eyes and without trying to speak, he nodded his head.

The family went on then, finishing their preparations for the outing. As they went out the door, Kate heard his light talker beeping. The computer voice said "I love you too."

He said that often. In fact, Kate could not remember a time even when they had been arguing over the children or debating some other matter of history, politics, or point of memory that he did not end the day by saying "I love you too" followed of course by "You're wrong."

They tried to talk him into sitting on the porch and watching the parade from there since the square was only two blocks away, but he didn't want to be on view, preferring to have his quiet time to think and bring his mood into line.

Chapter Thirty

Control

He had a certain concept of how he should behave, and being human, he sometimes lost control of the person he wanted to be. When this happened, he could see it and would withdraw into himself, trying to regain control. Rachel found his silence painful, always wanting to be there to talk him through it, to help him. This was not the man's way of doing things and so sometimes he would become so dark and brooding that she would pick a fight with him, making him spew out his anger. It was directed at her but beneath it all, she knew he had to reach the breaking point, letting the dam burst. His rage would ultimately bring him to the truth and they would become close again, as though they were once again falling in love.

Peace would return to him and he seemed to brace himself for another stand against his true enemy.

The same as everyone else........

They all sometimes forgot that Jim was ill during all of the busy days of life with a houseful of boys. He was treated as though he was the same as everyone else. The boys would gently move his hands for him and then complain because he told them to help their mother or to clean up their mess.

On one shameful occasion, Aaron became angry with Jim over some scolding and pushed his wheelchair into the back bedroom. He closed the door and left him there until Rachel discovered what he had done. Evidently Rachel was not as furious as Jim felt she should be about it, so he promptly told Kate when she arrived for her next visit. Kate landed on Aaron with the thundercloud approach and, immediately, Jim began to take up for Aaron.

Kate didn't mind and Jim was content. That's the way things were.

Jim, Rachel, and the boys were sometimes cruel to one another in their pain, and later, always apologetic. Human feelings, frustrations, anger, love, all had free reign in the Mitchell house.

Jim laughed at himself and joked with everyone about his condition. Everyone accused him of not playing fair when he was losing a debate and would say, "Now, wait a minute, you have to remember that I am a dieing man." It sounds strange to say now, but they always laughed at that and he enjoyed it more than anyone.

People sometimes asked how tall he was, since all of his new family and friends had only known him in the wheel chair. His answer was given with a chuckle. He would look down at his wheelchair and say, "Oh, about three feet don't you think?"

One of his favorite stories concerned an incident with one of his nurses in Houston, an incident he shared with only a few.

Jim had no privacy like everyone else. He could do nothing for himself, even the simplest things, the ones we all take for granted. The nurses bathed him and knew every inch of his body. In spite of this fact, he was a terrible flirt and could melt the most stoic prim female. He loved to recall the day his light talker cord became caught in his wheelchair. He called for the nurse and when she asked what was wrong he answered, "I'm hung."

He would smile a wide smile at this part of his story, his voice strained with laughter that couldn't come and say, "She just looked at me for a moment and said (with eyebrows raised) oh no you're not."

The room always erupted with laughter.

Kate often wondered exactly how many layers of pride had been peeled away from this young man over time as the illness overpowered him before he joined the Andersons. Certainly he had been proud of his physical strength and he had watched as his body deteriorated.

If only he could have seen himself through the family's eyes, he would have marveled at his own reflection, not recognizing the beauty of his soul as it covered him completely.

Chapter Thirty One

Financial solutions

Winter of 1990...

Financial problems had begun immediately after their marriage because of a glitch in Jim's nursing coverage. Jim's health insurance was one that had been connected to his last employer. After his disability, the out of state home office maintained his insurance coverage for a certain time period. When this ended, Jim's coverage was transferred to Texas (via a safeguard set in the policy to protect the company from prolonged disabilities such as Jim's). The transfer ended his nursing care coverage and the lifetime benefit became only $25,000. The only thing it took care of was prescription drugs at 80%. The premium for the policy was more than the benefits it paid each month. He was covered by Medicare which helped with his physical supplies like the wheelchair.

With the coverage cancelled for nursing Rachel could no longer work in Houston to bring in income for the family and Jim's income was only enough to cover his needs. The child support provided for Rachel's sons was also very small. A family of five could not live on their income. They were in a desperate situation.

Kate called government agencies asking about any assistance available. They did not qualify for food stamps, or other financial aid because their income placed them slightly above the government's poverty line for a family of five.

All of it was extremely frustrating because Rachel knew several families, couples who were in good health, who had more income each month, but received all kinds of assistance, including food stamps and welfare checks, plus Medicaid coverage. They explained how easy it was to get assistance but they had income they could hide. Rachel truthfully filled out all of the forms required and was told she could qualify for only $10 in food stamps.

Things couldn't get worse, or could they?

In the meantime, Jim's family was trying to help them to stay in their home and survive, but their wallet was not bottomless and something had to be done. Kate and Keith were not financially able to do more than buy groceries occasionally or pay a utility bill that had to be paid or else.

The young couple was desperately unhappy about their dilemma and finally Kate approached Jim about the possibility of selling his life insurance policy to make their life better and ease his worry. He had a life insurance policy with Rachel as the beneficiary. At first, he argued vehemently about cashing in the policy. Rachel argued that she would be able to take care of herself and the children later and he needn't worry about that. She had not married him for money. Why didn't it make more sense to use the insurance money while they needed it the most?

He finally agreed and then they began the long trail to selling the policy.

The first discovery of an impediment was that the beneficiary on his policy had not been changed from his first wife to Rachel. His brother Mike had sent in the forms but the insurance company did not follow his instructions. This brought about a complicated trail of paper and finally the beneficiary change.

Kate found several companies that bought life insurance

policies and success came at last in obtaining funds for the Mitchells to live on.

As was expected, the company that bought the policy took a huge hunk out of the face amount, but it was worth it to Rachel to see Jim happy and without worry over money. This way they did not have to accept money from Jim's family and could support themselves, keeping their lives as private as they wished.

Chapter Thirty Two

New things

Jim was like a child in a chocolate shop with the money. He felt so great about providing for his family. Rachel wanted to buy everything for him and he was the same about her. Some would say they should hold on to the funds and only use them as necessary. They looked at it differently. Jim's time was so short. This was to be all he had, all of the time they would have together, and they wanted it to be the best possible. The doctors had given Jim six months to live and the family would live those six months with great joy and not worry about where the money went.

Jim badly needed a new computer. That was one of the first things they bought.

The family went shopping in Houston. Jim wanted pretty dresses for Rachel and he beamed with pride each time she modeled one for him. She accepted only three. The boys were given anything they asked for. Rachel bought a special necklace for Jim. They bought simple wedding rings for each other and a new television was their final purchase on that trip.

Dining at the Olive Garden....

Andrew and Elyse were there with them and Jim sampled the taste of everything but did not swallow. He sat and beamed as everyone had a great time.

When Rachel arrived home she found a meatball in her purse....a souvenir of the meal at the Olive Garden, placed there by an unknown contributor. She left it on display for several days but it remained - unclaimed.

More new things..................

They renovated the house to a small degree, buying carpets for their floors, ceiling fans for every room, installed window heating and cooling conditioners, partially plumbed and wired the old house, making it comfortable. They could have purchased a new home but that would have taken all of the money. They needed funds to live on and decided to go the other route. They bought needed clothing, curtains and furniture including hutches for cabinets in the horrible kitchen, a dishwasher, and they paid off the two years remaining on the car note to alleviate all debts owed.

One of the major things Jim wanted to do was take the family on a vacation.

San Antone'.........autumn of 91

A long trip was out of the question with Jim's health. He required continual attention and the three boys were the same. Rachel could not bear the thought of a trip with all the added work and did not feel that she could stand up to the stress of chasing the boys, caring for Jim, driving and trying to find her way in a strange city, plus all that a vacation entails for a woman even under the best of circumstances. With this in mind, she and Jim invited Kate and her sister Elyse to go with them to San Antonio for a few days. This would add another child to the group with Andrew but the added women could help keep things under control and perhaps even Rachel would have fun on the trip.

It was decided that they would go to one of the best hotels on the river walk and take in the sites of historic San Antonio. From the moment they left the house, they were on a vacation and stopped at even familiar sites on the way as though they had never seen them before. They ate junk food, drank all the sodas they wanted, laughed and had a terrific time.

Rachel drove her car and Keith took the Anderson's car to add traveling space for kids and cargo, thus helping to reach their destination without war breaking out because of crowded conditions. He left the family at the hotel and returned home to care for the livestock on the farm.

The trip was totally, completely, wonderful.

The visit to the hotel almost began with a bang as they checked into their rooms at the Hyatt Regency. The adults in the group took their eyes off of Sean for a moment and he immediately began to examine a large thermostat on the wall in the lobby. With his penchant and innate ability to dismantle anything he desired, a few moments more and he would have disrupted their vacation and other guests as well. He never simply looked at things. His perpetual plan was to disassemble things and see how they worked. Rachel was able to reach him in time to replace the cover of the thermostat without the authorities noticing.

When they were given their room numbers, the boys asked which floor and headed at stampede speed for the line of elevator doors. They each got in a different elevator and began pushing buttons. Rachel ran after them in alarm, calling for a halt as she reached one of the doors and desperately tried to keep it from closing and sending her sons to oblivion somewhere in the hotel. Somehow, they managed to reach their rooms, including the boys who arrived at the end of their race. Jim managed to remain with the bunch and they had a few moments to collect themselves into some semblance of an organized team.

One of the great things about the hotel was its location within walking distance of the River Walk, the Alamo, the old Governor's mansion, the Tower of the Americas, the Institute of Texas Culture (where the kids all kissed the stuffed buffalo) and the shopping mall. They bought souvenirs, nothing major. Kate fell in love with a plastic coke can wearing sunglasses. It was dancing to the beat of music coming from the shop. Jim sent Rachel inside and bought it for her.

They asked passersby to take their photograph. Jim always wanted Rachel sitting in his lap.

As with so many things, they enjoyed the day.

They leased a car and spent a second day at the Zoo at Breckenridge Park. The boys rode the train and played for a while in the paddle boats before everyone cooked to a nice bronze while viewing all of the menagerie housed at the zoo. The next day's schedule included Sea World, probably Jim's favorite place. He had always loved the ocean and seeing the whales and dolphins was a reminder of that.

About midafternoon, Rachel, Elyse and the boys left Jim and Kate at the whale pool while they went for one of the water rides. Kate's memory of it was sitting quietly there in the shade of the canopy with Jim. He began to laugh and she joined him when she saw them. Kate's mother had a habit of using the term "drowned rats" which came to her mind immediately. The four boys were jumping with joy at being so wet but Rachel and Elyse had that drowned rat expression on their faces, their clothes pasted against their bodies, long hair now plastered to their heads.

They could have bathed in Vaseline petroleum jelly and looked about the same.

The boat ride on the river and dinner there topped off the last day.

They reached a roadblock for Jim when they started to board the river boat because the boat had no wheelchair access ramps. Jim looked at the family with a disappointed expression and told them to go on without him. That definitely was not going to happen and as they discussed the problem among themselves, a strong man suddenly appeared and without a word, lifted Jim onto the boat, wheelchair and all.

Sadly, he didn't give his name. Whoever or wherever you are, if you read this and remember, know that you were an angel that day.

The quiet ride on the river was beautiful and peaceful. They wanted it to last forever. The boat floated along in the evening shadows, moving beneath and away from the noise of the city streets above them. Bridges overhead glowed with soft lights and the windows of office buildings became stars overhead. The shops and sidewalk cafés were alive with music and laughter as other families celebrated their own joy with living. Even Rachel's boys sat quietly absorbing those very special moments.

The little caravan returned to the hotel, even though they hated for any of the fun to end, but the day wasn't over yet. Swimming at the pool, movies in the room and more room service (desserts all around) were the best part of each evening with everyone musing about the day's events.

Rachel gave Jim his Ensure before every meal so mealtime would not be so difficult for him. He could not swallow but he tasted his favorite things in minute amounts, held them in his mouth for a while and asked Rachel to rinse his mouth after each taste. The boys questioned him about not being able to eat. He always said he didn't mind.

The trip was over too soon. Keith rejoined them for the final leg of the journey and the family headed home.

A stop in Sequin with Keith's parents gave them a chance to share the events of the trip. Jim made his way into their hearts the same as he did the rest of the Andersons. In later years, a favorite memory of Jim and Keith's dad would be of their **Thanksgiving together at the farm.**

The family had gathered for the celebration in Fayetteville that year. The family was scattered here and there about the big farmhouse with most of the group in the living room, collected in front of the fireplace. The kids were romping about the yard, their laughter and squeals, and the crowing of the roosters was coming in through the windows on the sun porch.

Dad and Jim were sitting in the kitchen. Keith's dad was very hard of hearing and Jim struggled with his light talker, turning the volume up as much as possible to make Dad hear him. Finally, Kate heard their laughter and went in to share the fun.

They were still laughing when Kate asked what had happened.

Jim said, "I just told Dad that with his difficulty hearing and my difficulty talking, we weren't getting a whole lot said."

The family finished that day sitting around the kitchen table competing in a long game of Trivial Pursuit. It resulted in Elyse, Rachel and Jim in a giant struggle for the Championship. Kate could not recall which of them became the victor. The most memorable thing about it was the exchange of jokes and fun with everyone laughing and learning who Rachel's Jim was.

Chapter Thirty Three

Sean's poem about the trip to San Antonio

My fourth poem...."San Antone"
                              October 13, 1991

It's fun to be in San Antone'
As people stroll on the river walk
I listen as they talk
They chatter about "the beautiful river"
And touring boats go drifting by
Children run up and down the walk
And the parents eat their pie
Tourists take pictures of family and friends
So they can remember San Antone'

Across the street in a quiet place
Is a shrine called the Alamo
Where brave men died for Texas
Many years ago
They fought in an awful battle
Fought to the bitter end
The silent past now holds the sound
Of the mighty cannon's roar
But I think I heard it yesterday once more
In the town called San Antone'

Chapter Thirty Four

T'wer the Night

Rachel often said that getting the boys off to school was like playing bumper cars. They could never find their clothes, homework, books, shoes, coats, or the correct time to leave the house. It made no difference if things were laid out in tidy bundles the night before. Those bundles had disappeared to parts unknown before morning.

Since Sean seldom slept, everything in his room was usually cowering beneath what appeared to be an explosion of encyclopedias required for one of his research projects and that school stuff got in his way. The toothbrushes were under some unidentified party's bed and the combs and brushes were probably hanging from a tree limb. Even with all of this, homework was the biggest trial of school days for Mother. Every evening, hours of struggle produced only partially completed work, which was usually the wrong page, or became hopelessly lost somewhere in the house(the dog could not have possibly found the homework to eat it so he could never be blamed).

Always willing to add to the mix whenever possible, Jim agreed to almost anything the boys wanted. On one occasion, he almost went to school to be the subject of show and tell for Sean. Very proud of his new dad, he wanted to show him off. He also wanted to explain to his friends about ALS. Kate didn't think it was such a bad idea but Rachel had two distracted boys to prepare for the school day and she didn't want to have to take the entire family…meaning Patrick would have to go too if Jim did. So, he didn't make it to school with Sean after all. It would have been a great lesson for the students.

Christmas was coming and what to do for the boys was a problem…

Knowing they loved being someone other than themselves, Rachel suggested costumes. The Andersons had an old trunk and this was to become a treasure chest which would hold leather carpenters belts, scarves of all materials and colors, gloves, hats, masks, more belts and Kate would add capes, pants, and tops made of vinyl, metallic silver polyester, and jewels fit for any pirate who ever sailed the seven seas. A few plastic swords were purchased and the prize was ready.

Rachel and Jim bought numerous gifts for all but the gift the family loved most was a poem they wrote called…

..T'wer the Night Before Christmas..

By Rachel and Jim Mitchell (Mr. and Mrs. …thank you)

T'wer the night before Christmas and all through the house
The three boys were stirring…and…the cat we call Mouse.
The stockings we'd hung by the chimney this year
The boys had them on…part of strange spaceman gear.

The house was a shambles, the windowpanes shook
Charlie squawked from his cage
                    And got whacked with a book.
Jim in his wheelchair, and Mom on the floor

Yelled, Boys, get to bed. We can't stand anymore!

"Santa won't stop by here with all of this strife.
It's like a war zone, he'd fear for his life.
When outside the house, we heard such a crash
We thought that a varmint was raiding the trash.

It was Santa himself in his usual suit
Except, now he wore Nike's and an earring to boot.
His eyes still twinkled, he was still round and fat
But this modern day Santa was one cool cat.

My stars, what a racket, he said with a shout.
You scared Rudolph so, his nose almost went out.
Now, how would it look to fly without lights?
I might hit a plane on this cold winter night?

Now, where is my list, I must check it twice
The one that I keep on who's naughty and nice?
You boys have been busy, the list is quite long,
I can tell by your faces, you're hoping I'm wrong.

First there is Aaron, my wily young con,
Flimflamming your brothers to do something wrong.
Once the deed has been done and your mom is just frantic,
You stand by dumbfounded as if shocked by their antics.

I see that you've learned how to drive your mom's car,
We can be thankful you didn't go far

I should also remind you, get this into your head
Dishes belong in the kitchen, not under your bed.

And to Sean the Wizard, who's never quite dressed
Please try my young friend, not to make such a mess.
All your potions, and projects, the rocks you hold dear
Dirty socks you've had stashed in your room for a year.

It's a nice thing to do, when you wash your mom's car
But with windows rolled UP, it works better by far
I do not advise dives in a tub overflowing
Or 6 a.m. battle cries, war whoops or crowing."

And now to young Patrick, who is so full of fight
The time for your battles is not late at night
Don't carry poor Phoebe around in a sack
One day she'll get angry and give you a smack.

And remember, each morning, when you get out of bed,
That you're really not sick. It's all in your head.
You're a bit of a wolf, a midget Don Juan.
Why not wait till first grade, to come on so strong?

When all's said and done, you are wonderful boys.
Kind hearted and sweet, you give all of us joy.
It's true, you've been toots, but no need to be sad
For there's a lot of new toys here, to drive Mom and Jim
mad.

Now, I must go, I've got lots more to do.
I still have to visit your cousin Andrew.
The boys were excited, their eyes all aglow
They really didn't want Santa to go.

We gathered round the window, as he got ready to leave,
The boys were so happy, and a little …. relieved
As we watched the sleigh climb up into the night
We heard, Cowabonga Dudes, and to all a goodnight.

Jim and Rachel

AKA- Jimani

The references made throughout the Christmas tale were based on reality.

Chapter Thirty Five

Pets

Two of the family cats were mentioned in the poem but there were more. One scraggly one was called. S.O., short for screen ornament since the screen door was his favorite place and he preferred to wait there on a continual basis. He didn't meow like a normal cat and produced something not unlike the sound of a buzzer. Stubborn, he insisted that he belonged in the house and since he wasn't admitted, his plan was to make someone feel pretty darn guilty about it. Phoebe went around sleeping on Patrick's neck and would have been in his pocket if possible. Mouse was a house decoration, little more.

The present dog was a shaggy black poodle mix named Einstein. Sean must have held the upper hand in the naming, but the mutt had a difficult time remembering even his name and was in no way comparable to his namesake. The boys loved him just the same.

The car washing..........

Another learning milestone came when Sean, in one of his rare moments of concern over his share of the work load, decided to wash the car with windows rolled down. All of this was on his own volition.

When his parents noticed what he was doing the car was already well soaked, inside and out. Another twist to the washing was that Sean had selected fabric softener instead of soap. It smelled better and sudsy dishwashing liquid was old hat. Car doors were opened and a waterfall ensued.

No one could recall how long it took for the seats and carpets to dry but the car smelled divine.

A driving lesson for Aaron...

Aaron quickly did his part. He added his touch to the car and almost the house they lived in. Being the oldest, he could do nothing less. He decided he could drive as well as anyone he knew and so he confidently began to move the car out of the way so they could use the basketball goal. He moved it quickly and far enough with the door still ajar to rip the car door from its hinges and almost collapse the car port by removing the center post which was holding the roof in place.

The cost of repairs on the car alone was almost $2,000. That was an expensive basketball game but Aaron's work was much more effective than what Sean had done.

Snow.....???

Rachel and Jim had to keep a watchful eye out all the time for their brood. Sean occupied a large share of the watch. On one occasion, he decided that clothes washing detergent was intriguingly close to snow. This became too much to bear without a test. The result was an amazing snowfall in his room. His test was a complete success.

He was able to blanket every minute inch of the large room by using an entire box of Tide. He proudly explained his method, telling Kate that he perched himself near the top of the bookcase to make the snowfall simulate reality. He was even quite willing to repeat the process for her to see. She refused but it would have been a sight to warm a mother's heart. Kate completely missed out on those special effects as Rachel removed most of the evidence before she reached the scene.

You won't believe what Sean has done.......

When these events occurred, Rachel usually made a desperate call to her mother which always began, "Mother, you won't believe what Sean has done now." But she was wrong there. At this point, Kate would believe anything.

When he was only two, Sean removed the doors from the pantry in the kitchen and painted the television set, plus a large portion of the living room carpet to please his mother. As luck would have it, he used water based paint. Rachel was fortunate indeed.

The roof...........

All three of the boys became added trouble when they discovered a ladder leading up into the loft. This was located in the infamous kitchen pantry which also housed the water heater. This access to the roof was a stealth squad's dream.

The roof provided a wide lookout surface, an excellent human lightening rod test area, one's own private observatory for star gazing, nude sunbathing, and if the door of the pantry was blocked off, a perfect island to isolate Patrick from them when he was being troublesome. Upon gazing from this lofty height, out toward the pecan trees behind the house, they immediately realized that they had no alternative but to build a diving pit in the back yard.

Anyone would have thought so.

This pit was prepared by digging a good sized hole and filling it with water. Water, plus dirt, plus boys wrestling produced a mud pit and this was soon put to use as the most wonderful of daring experiences. This pit gave them the capability of slipping off the edge of the roof at precisely the right point and destroying enemies around the pit with one single filthy splash.

Patrick.........and the duct tape

The isolation of Patrick happened in various ways. On one occasion, mother and grandmother went to town for groceries leaving the boys attending one another and Jim. Upon arriving home with the usual huge load of groceries, all seemed well. Kate went on home after Rachel's things were unloaded. Of course, they had noted a strange behavior from Sean and Aaron. Instead of ravaging through the bags of food, they immediately disappeared to points unknown.

Kate was in the midst of packing her things away when she received a call from Rachel. Guess what?

"Just tell me. What now?"

"It's Patrick again...they got him."

She explained that she had started hearing a loud thump from somewhere...which turned out to be Sean's room. When she investigated, she found a very large ball of silver duct tape rolling around in the cedar closet. The tape was an item she purchased on every trip to town for the boys to use in their construction projects. This time, they had covered Patrick's mouth with the tape, then proceeded to make a cocoon with their pesky little brother inside. Both Rachel and Kate were alarmed about this and had a long talk with the boys about the dangers of such things and how Patrick could have smothered. Throughout his life, Patrick felt he was never able to get even with his big brothers for that one.

A rainy spell...........

When rain sets in for a number of days in succession, the ground becomes soaked and if the temperature is right, the phenomenon that is a delight to all children occurs. The mud suddenly gives birth to millions of minute frogs. The wonderful slimy things are a miracle that has to be saved for posterity. When this great event occurred in Fayetteville and was discovered, the boys grabbed mother's pots and pans and ran outside. They didn't have a second to lose.

Rachel knew they were happily collecting frogs and believed this was no reason for concern. She was allowing herself something she seldom had, a time to rest. Meanwhile, the boys decided that the containers they were using were never going to be sufficient to collect the number of frogs they required. So, they began dumping the pots and buckets of frogs in Sean's bedroom and running out for more. Somewhere, far into their project, Rachel noticed a tiny green frog on the floor in front of her chair. As she stared at him, he was joined by a second hopping creature and then a third as the frogs explored their new home. She looked over her shoulder and the trail to the source was evident. Frogs were gleefully greeting one another and discussing their new premises beginning at the door to Sean's room.

Rachel failed to count the exact number they collected during the following week but she said it was considerable.

Everything had to be shared with Jim.....

The backyard was a favorite gathering place for fireflies in the late spring. As with all children, the boys gathered these beautiful unfortunate creatures in jars and took them into the house to share with Jim. Kate went over to visit the next afternoon after one such harvest and Rachel was still grumbling about all the bugs in the house. As she finished speaking, they heard Jim laughing in the living room. He was sitting in his chair by the computer, wearing his standard hot day attire which was a long T shirt and cotton men's under shorts. This was perfectly proper and decent clothing for him to wear.

The women and the boys ran into the room and asked him what was so funny. He nodded his head toward his lap and said, "I believe I've just found, or caught another firefly, either that or I've developed a new symptom."

There in his lap, flashing from the inside front of his shorts was the innocent firefly who had lost its way. The boys scrambled to catch it and Jim became frantic, looking at Rachel for help. Kate quickly left the room and listened to the laughter as the luckless bug was retrieved.

When Kate rejoined the group Jim grinned at her with a twinkle in his eye and said, "That one must have been a female."

Einstein.......

The trouble with the older bad boys of Fayetteville continued throughout these months.

Since the Catholic Church was at the end of Bell Street which ran in front of the Mitchell house, traffic was always heavy on days when activities were going on there. When church was over, a group of the local boys drove about town in an old pickup truck, taunting others and feeding their egos. One of the habits these boys had was to try to run over anything or anyone in the street. Finally, they were successful in front of the Mitchell house. They managed to run over Einstein as he stood beside the road. He was not in the street, but they swerved to hit him and drove away laughing while the little helpless dog yelped and writhed in pain beneath the street light.

Rachel called her father and he raced into town to see about Einstein. They found him in agony and very near death. His body was badly mangled and he was not going to survive. Keith was prepared. He took his twenty two rifle and ended Einstein's pain.

The turmoil in the house was intense. Keith quickly gave the boys a job to do. He helped them as they prepared the grave. Wrapped the family pet in a blanket and buried him, a last gesture of love for an innocent little dog.

Recovery......the boxer...summer of 91

After this happened, Jim's mother decided to give the family a boxer puppy. Jim had once had one that he loved and as always, they wanted to help. This act of kindness inadvertently brought about the loss of another beloved family pet.

There was no way to have known that the gift would be a problem. However, the pup was big, clumsy, and I'm sorry to say, apparently stupid. With his monstrous feet, he tore through every screen door that exited at his level and soon gaping holes were in the one on the west side of the living room and another in Sean's room.

........baby blue jay

Into this situation, Aaron delivered an orphaned baby blue jay and began raising it as his own. The bird recognized Aaron as "the one with the food". He began to flutter his wings and cheep loudly every time Aaron came into the room. The featherless mom would grin proudly, pick up the tweezers and dutifully stuff a few morsels of juicy dog food down the throat of his grateful charge. This bird grew strong and healthy and quickly sprouted the feathers he needed to fly. He began to fly about the house in his faltering fashion and was sometimes underfoot. The boys decided the house had to be declared off limits to the cats and everyone was on constant guard when the doors were opened.

The young bird finally had to be secluded in Aaron's room. At some point during one late night, someone left the door to Aaron's room ajar. About midmorning, the flock began to stir and Aaron immediately missed his little jay. A search of the house found the door on the north side open, and cats inside the house, along with the stupid boxer, but no baby jaybird. They searched for a single feather but found none.

The final hopeful conclusion was that the baby had found the opening in one of the screens, escaped safely, and flown away to freedom.

They never knew for certain, but one blue jay always stayed close to the house and Aaron thought he looked at him in a special way.

Love thy neighbor.....

To the dismay of the neighbors, who often stared at the house from behind bushes which did not conceal their location, the boys did whatever came to mind. They fought with buckets of water, sodas, and Rachel also bought cans of shaving soap for the boys to have shaving cream fights on the front porch.

They raised another disturbance by camping out in the front yard in the tent Jim bought them. This was all night fun while it lasted but the boxer puppy ended that by eating the tent.

The boys didn't appreciate it but the neighbors probably did.

Chapter Thirty Six

X spouse

Rachel's X came once a month to pick up the three older boys even though the divorce said he was to have them every two weeks. He sometimes forgot that he was no longer the man of Rachel's house and said things he shouldn't. These two, who had shared their sons and bad memories had always talked to one another like gasoline and a burning match. They often argued when he came. On one occasion, the X was in the kitchen spouting words to Rachel that set Jim off.

He raised his voice to its loudest pitch and ordered the X into his presence. With eyes flashing with rage, he informed the guilty party as to his location, a place in which Jim resided as the reigning man of the house. The X stood quietly, as if on the verge of bowing to a Monarch, while he was read the rules he was to abide by in the future.

When the X was leaving, Jim watched from his position near the front windows, he glowered in such a way that he somehow reminded Kate of a rooster ready for a fight.

This was the last time Rachel heard harsh words from the X within Jim's earshot.

Chapter Thirty Seven

Tranquility?

In recent years the boys have told of some of the things they did without the parents' knowledge. Now that the danger is past they feel secure in revealing some of the truth. They say they had ways of getting even with one another (and sometimes others), usually at night for battles lost during the daytime. Patrick, being the smallest had the most to get even about and so he was actively involved. They mixed potions and poured those in their sleeping victims' mouths (Sean may have received the worst dose) or waited until Aaron, who was the lark of the family and thus the earliest to doze, was peacefully resting. Then the surprise attack was on.

Rachel and Jim were not ignored in this middle of the night fun and often suffered loss of sleep as well.

Sean woke one morning to find his room almost impassable. His brothers had made good use of Mother's dental floss. Rachel commented that it was amazing how much floss is in one of those tiny packets or maybe two. 'She said the room was almost solid with the white string crossing wall to wall and back again.

The boys also removed the screens to their bedroom windows to allow fast exits during scraps. Some of their friends found these exit/entrances convenient and joined them in late night adventures in the pasture behind the house and probably many more places they have left out of the telling.

Jim was a good scout.......

If Jim had been able, he would have been right in the middle of all of this mayhem, and probably witnessed a large portion of it. Regardless, it was good medicine for him. If nothing else, it was an effective distraction.

A night of reckoning .....

The bullies who came to their yard uninvited eventually learned their place. On a dark night, unspoken about at the time, one - I dare you situation too many - sent Aaron into the house for his baseball bat. He cleared the yard of the intimidators and soon all three boys were using whatever it took to control their own domain. They were learning that Patrick's philosophy was often the best one to follow when it came to certain types of people. Over time, the three brothers became taller than all of their adversaries and when that happened even the drive-bys decreased in frequency. Aaron took care of those by waiting behind trees with his baseball bat for the opportunity to take out a few windows on the tough boys' trucks. Sean thought a brick would suffice just as well and Patrick was armed with both (meaning a brick and a baseball bat). Whether their diligence ever paid off or not remains one of the family mysteries.

There was another antagonist who was not included in the active bully category. He was a boy who rode by the house on his bike calling names. He was wise enough not to stop and let things go farther. Patrick returned barb for barb in the name calling and one of the names in his wide vocabulary was the favorite for this boy…"Watermelon Head". Every time Kate scolded Patrick for saying that, he swore to her…"scouts honor, Grama" that the name was appropriate and she would fully agree if she ever saw this phantom nemesis.

This was to be another missed opportunity.

Chapter Thirty Eight

Skits

On August 2, 1990, Jim called the family in to see the news on TV. The boys became excited as they watched the firefight in Kuwait. It was the real thing. America was at war.

This was history as it happened and Jim told the boys, "You are seeing it live. It's something you will be able to tell your grandchildren. "After that day, the family made a habit of gathering around when the news came on showing what was going on in Kuwait.

Toward the end of the war, February 28, 1991, Iraqi soldiers were running for cover and surrendering in massive numbers, the road back to Baghdad was filled with armored equipment and ragged soldiers returning home.

The family was relieved when it was announced that the conflict was at an end. The violence had to stop. The Iraqi's seemed totally defenseless. Sadam had not surrendered but the death and destruction was a horrible thing to see.

Jim felt the boys needed to be aware that war games were not about having a good time. It was very serious and when they became men it could possibly be a part of their future.

During this time period, Sadam Hussein became a favorite of the boys' comedy routines or skits with "the mother of all this and that "prevalent in the dialogue. Their expertise growing, they decided to record something.

Rachel and Jim listened from the family room while the boys worked next door in the living room. Patrick was the sound man in charge of the recorder. Aaron was the major player and also the director. Fights erupted occasionally during the taping when little brother forgot to turn the machine on or off at the right moment or Sean stumbled at his reading. In order to really get into the characters, they dressed appropriately for the parts. In this instance, weapons were strapped on their persons, berets (or semblance thereof) were worn, and boots. Aaron (Sadam Hussein) who had the idea, and Sean, the author of course, began to read their parts.

It went *something* like this. Aaron began…flawlessly going through his part and Sean who had the tendency to mumble, would fumble and mumble his response.

"I am the General,"… (Aaron)

"and I am your guard." (Raspy voiced Sean)

"I wear the pants."

"And they're loaded with lard."

"Iraq is my country."

"And we are your slaves?"

"I drink lots of beer."

"But it's women that he craves."

"We are the conquerors."

"The mothers of all fools."

"We don't give a damn"…

"about anybody's rules."

"I am going to **take** - **all** the world's **oil**"…

" but … our tanks, (squeaky voice) they are made of aluminum foil!"

"Yes, I am the General as you can see." …

" ……. (Loud laugh) (**ha ha**) but - all of your children look a lot like me."

"Ten Hut!"

This was to end with the clicking of heels, double fisted chest banging, and a loud...in unison **"Hyuh!"**

This recording session went on --- and on--- starting over and over, and over and over.... as they rehearsed and gradually worked their way through the routine. At long last, after intense frustration with Sean for not coming in on time and Patrick screwing up with the recorder, and too much laughter in the serious? places, Sean read his part with perfection down to the point of Aaron's final "Ten Hut!" yell. But there was dead silence followed by a burst of laughter.

Aaron was so surprised and dumbfounded by Sean's success when it finally came that he missed his cue at the end of what would have been a perfect routine. Laughter instead of success had to be good enough. They gave up and the project was scrubbed. Sadly, their wonderful recording that Rachel managed to save was lost somewhere in the family's time vault.

Pakistani store clerk....

They sometimes practiced their Pakistani Convenience Store Operator's accent with a discussion between the two (Aaron and Sean) Aaron was the Pakistani behind the counter. Sean was the customer. One sequence was based on the fact that cigarettes were simply "not to be sold to children" under penalty of law, a fine, loss of license to sell these items, and **"heaven forbidt**, jail time." the belligerent customer (Sean) was informing the cashier of the difficulties he would face with his mother's ire (he was very descriptive here) if he returned home without these articles. "It is not against the law in Fayetteville for you to sell me these cigarettes. **No, it is not...not in Fayetteville."** Meanwhile, the very thick tongued proprietor decides the customer is **"Callink"** him a liar. "I am **not** a liar. I tell you to your **ugly face. I yam nodt a liar."** The argument deteriorated into who exactly first called who a liar, total disgust with one another - and a tremendous amount of spitting was produced in the conversation.

ABC News Interview...Another such display representing their opinion of current events or news footage was an interview of Arafat by Sam Donaldson went something like this.

Aaron was the ABC news interviewer (hair pasted down appropriately) and Sean (dressed for the occasion of course with towel on his head, bathrobe etc.) was Yassir Yourafart. An overcooked frankfurter was the microphone. The mustachioed Palestinian acted *true to his name* and kept interrupting in various(?) ways. Patrick was the sound effects man for this also with Yassir reacting with facial 'grimaces etc while Patrick made noises in a plastic juice bottle. Mr. Donaldson was having difficulty calming Yassir down for the discussion and finally told him if he didn't stop his outrageous behavior as well as demanding all of the continent of Africa and the Island of Greece he was going to find himself being questioned by non-other than Barbara Walters. Arafat immediately fell into line.

The pure comedic genius of these routines and the laughter they produced gave wonderful moments to the family and Jim loved every minute of it.

Chapter Thirty Nine

Tell me Sherlock

Ideas that popped into Sean's head were sometimes alarming.

It was about this time when Sean decided that the world presented many more opportunities than those existing within their household. He placed a piercing eye upon the town bank. Sean's plan was to accomplish the perfect bank intrusion, a caper that would make him famous for his shrewd deductions. This would not be in the order of making money. This was to be a perfectly planned breach of the bank's security. He would expose the weakness he saw in the system and make it a safer place for the people's money.

The problem was, he was having difficulty locating that weak point. He tried to discuss his ideas with Rachel and put forth the premise of entering the bank through the night deposit box...yes it was small but perhaps he could remove the said device. There was also the prospect of a tunnel or a wall collapse via Cufr's Dry Goods store next to the bank.

Rachel was appalled at these suggestions and promptly refused to talk about such a thing as breaking into a bank with her son. "First of all, Sean, a super brain future thief does not talk about his *plans* for illegal activities with anyone, much less his own mother."

Women, particularly moms, were a puzzlement to Sean.

When he discussed his ideas with Kate, she simply pointed out the holes in his approach to the problem. As imperfect as they are, Grandmas still try not to discourage their grandchildren about anything.

Later, Rachel and Jim had a quiet talk with Sean about the laws of the land, what represented a breach of laws, and the consequences of certain actions, including those involving research projects.

He accepted the facts as presented to him, but just the same, grownups took all of the fun out of life. Sean wasn't sure he ever wanted to be one.

Chapter Forty

Chicken vengeance

After Jim and Rachel were married, the long trips to work in Houston for sequences of three days were out of the question, so Rachel took a job working nights in a nursing home in LaGrange. She first hired a young woman from Fayetteville to take care of Jim and her boys.

This didn't work out because the house, boys, and Jim were too much for the woman and she was not suited for the job. Rachel had to let her go. The woman became angry and though there was no proof of who actually did it, the Mitchell's soon found a dead chicken hanging over their door. Someone said it was a local insult.

The family didn't mind the insult but felt very bad for the innocent chicken.

Chapter Forty One

Socks on the Ceiling Fan

A letter with the first page missing......

Rachel wrote many letters that never found their way to the mailbox. These lay about the house among many heaps of papers and sometimes Kate found them and saved words more precious than she could have known at the time.

Rachel often wrote of the boy's rambunctious behaviors and other things they did. In putting away their clothes she sometimes described their efforts as ending with socks on the ceiling fans, tied in minute knots because the fans had been running when the socks were filed away there. There actually were, socks on her ceiling fans in little knots so she hadn't exaggerated.

Page two.....Rachel's letter to Mary.

I was so lucky to find Jim. He tells me that I'm beautiful when I look like I've been crawling around under the house, and he accepts PMS as a reasonable excuse for the checkbook not being balanced, or he is too smart to push the point. He can be very considerate and romantic. I am coming out better in his book than I am in true life, although he has refused to describe me as angelic or saint-like, no matter how much I nibble on his ear as he's writing. If he catches me reading over his shoulder he has an irritating habit of writing something really obscene. It would serve him right if he accidentally left one of those cute, twisted little remarks in and it was published that way. That strong will that is so infuriating when we fight has also been a blessing- he doesn't let his illness get the best of him; there are times that you have to remind him that he is ill so he won't push himself too far. We are able to lead a fairly normal life, and forget at times what may be ahead of us and it is to his credit, because if I start thinking ahead too far he gets very optimistic and playful, (or frisky - my personal favorite). His doctors have become apathetic by this point, so we are on our own for the most part. Jim has to watch me like a hawk because I am forever trying to sneak some new miracle cure into this feedings, sea plants and vegetable juices, and I think he is afraid that if I hear that pureed garden slugs have healing properties I might be trying to slip them in on him. He is really off base on where the real danger lies. He doesn't realize how many times I have almost given him my hormone pills by mistake. That would surely give him a whole new perspective.

My boys are growing so fast. Aaron is 10 going on 30, big for his age, and the most belligerent, sassy mouth imaginable...Mother says he takes after me???

Sean is eccentric, but since he is oblivious to everything going on around him it doesn't seem to bother him in the least. He gets along great with everybody (except Patrick, who he would gladly trade off for a dead snake), but he is happiest when he is off by himself, making secret potions or taking things apart. He is so preoccupied that he is constantly in trouble at school because he is disrupting the class with sound effects or simply getting out of his seat and wandering off, forgetting about class altogether. He makes straight A's. Pretty good for a kid who could walk out of his shoes and never realize it.

Patrick is very handsome (he thinks. And I agree...an

impartial judgment on my part). He is such a little wolf at 5 that he has me worried. Especially since he seems to be partial to older women. He is feisty. This trait has the two older boys looking forward to him starting school this next year because when he gets angry, he is like a badger, he just won't give up. "Back off or I'll sick my little brother on you". He is so persistent in seeking revenge that I have caught him ambushing one of his brothers after they have gone to sleep at night in retaliation for something they did to him during the day.

We have been on an Arnold Schwarzenegger movie binge since school let out. They are all speaking with an Austrian accent, doing a lot of swaggering with toy machine guns and knives stuck in their waistbands and socks…jumping on their bikes with the warning…"I'll be back". They spent a week after they watched the Ten Commandments standing on the coffee table wrapped in bed sheets, leading the slaves out of Egypt. Patrick got tired of the game very quickly… he always had to be a camel.

We have been very happy here in Podunk Ville where we will never be totally inconspicuous. We weren't born *here, we aren't Czech or Catholic, and we are not related to at least half of the other inhabitants. The last town scandal was when a handful of local teenagers (That's how many teenagers live here, a handful) got a little drunk and took the fire truck for a joyride. They actually had to bring a deputy in from LaGrange for a couple of weeks to settle things down. The people here don't get in a hurry to do anything. If you hire someone to fix something, they may get to it this week, might not. It seems like the weather has to be just right, not too hot...too cold and the wind blowing from the right direction. If they get tired they take a nap at any point in the construction. You don't complain too much as the customer since they are still charging 1927 rates....and you might pay them today, but if you get tired....*

I would send you a picture of my boys but I haven't been able to catch all three boys unmarred at the same time. I am going to try to put a ban on self-done haircuts, brother-bashing, and tattoos and/or gruesome scars painted on with permanent markers until I can get them all reasonably unmarked at the same time...however, the phrase "when pigs fly" comes to mind there.

Chapter Forty Two

Do you want a mint?

Rachel had a tendency to not be able to make up her mind. An example of this that the family refers to often, happened over a simple question. "Do you want a mint?" They were on their way to buy groceries in LaGrange. Rachel was tired and talking about other things, Jim and the boys mostly. Kate asked her a second time before she put the mints away. "Do you want a mint?" Rachel said yes and as Kate handed one to her, Rachel changed her mind. Kate put the mints back in her purse but as she did, Rachel said, "Oh well, maybe I will." Kate took the mints out of her purse and began peeling back the paper. Rachel sighed, "Oh, I don't think so after all, Mother." So, Kate resignedly rewrapped the mints and returned them to her purse. No sooner were they there than Rachel spoke again. "Mother, I think I actually do want one." Kate quietly reached in her purse and removed the mints. Rachel started to speak and Kate began to laugh. "Baby, listen closely. Do you want a mint or not?" and so the tradition began.

When family members can't make up their mind about anything, someone always says, "Do you want a mint?"

Kick butt coffee….

Rachel lived on strong coffee, really strong coffee. She increased the strength of this brew as time passed and her exhaustion overwhelmed her. It became a tradition for her sons to make her first pot of coffee (and then it became every pot of coffee) to help kick start her day. Kate watched the process that was explained by the boys. The coffee grounds should "fill the filter cup to the brim". This was Mom's kick-butt coffee.

Vinegar girl…..

Sweet and kind, hot tempered and difficult, this was Rachel. She was a person like everyone else with good and bad habits and always late for every occasion. She said whatever came into her mind, sometimes pleasant, sometimes not, but she was the best friend anyone could have and Kate loved her beyond all reasoning. She called her, her vinegar girl because she was not perfect but the nearest thing to perfection a mother could ever want in a daughter, you see, vinegar is - almost wine. That was Rachel.

Chapter Forty Three

January 20, 1992...A letter from Jim's mother

Dear Jim,

I already knew everything you wrote in your letter. Call it intuition, ESP, or maybe that invisible connecting thread there is between people who love each other - but I knew almost everything. Difficulty with your speech was evident, of course, and I assumed breathing would next become a labor. If you are right, and I have been in any way a good influence on your amazing will power, then I am thankful. I, too, am remembering standing by your hospital bed and trying to will you to breathe. I don't know which of us is responsible for your recovery then, I just wish we could be so successful now. As for your relationship with grandmother, both when you were a child and now, I am so grateful she had you and you had her love and understanding. I suppose I was always the mother/father disciplinarian back then so thank goodness for grandmother. Later, when you had become a grown man and left Houston to spend a few months here with us, I think our relationship changed. Remember how we would both look forward to 5:00 pm when Rita left and we'd have time to talk? Both of us were always disappointed when Buddy got home too soon for us to finish our visit - those talks were the highlights of my days back then.

I wish you wouldn't feel you'd be spoiling my visits with you by being honest about what's going on. I sense most things anyway and it would not be possible to spoil a visit. I know I see far too little of you and I'd give anything to be able to visit more often and stay longer. However, things here with grandmother really tie me down - and even to the point where I rarely go to the farm any more. I haven't misled you about her though. She's very weak, tires easily, so that even helping to put groceries away exhausts her, and she has very bad emphysema. She is afraid to be off the oxygen for more than an hour at a *time, though I have noticed she can survive much longer if she has something going on around her that she's interested in and if she doesn't exert herself. Part of the problem, then, is psychological, and this is because she is pretty much alone. All her brothers and sisters are gone, and I am truly all the family she has now – at least I'm the only one close by. She worries about me constantly and is afraid something will happen to me. Fortunately, she really likes Shirley, who stays with her during the week, but Shirley is now having severe financial difficulties and we may lose her if she can find a job that pays more. Shirley cannot spend the night so that I can be gone as she has a daughter and grandchild to take care of at home. So....for me to get away, Val has to come stay with grandmother....but.....then I'd be driving to Fayetteville alone and both Buddy and grandmother would worry themselves to death. Now I'm the gal who has driven alone all over Texas and indeed, the U.S.A., and now it seems no one considers me capable of doing what I've always done! Actually, I do understand. I guess I'm pretty valuable in grandmothers and Buddy's eyes and they* worry about me. They worry too much so that sometimes I feel trapped but at the same time, I understand. To make a long story shorter, it's easier to get Val to come with me (which she always wants to do) and make the trip in one day. I hope all of this helps you to understand my predicament.

Thank God for Rachel - whimsical, earthy, strong, caring, crazy, unpredictable, dependable, witty, creative, and bone-tired Rachel. Without her, your life would have been nothing more than a growing void. I, too, worry about her where both the physical and psychological factors of being a "caregiver" are concerned. I wish we were just a little closer geographically so I could be of some help, but you have to remember, Jim, hers are labors of love. I hope you are better where your cold in concerned. I got your letter Saturday afternoon and didn't call you then as I was so emotional, I cried over everything. Then, I tried to call you yesterday (Sunday) and got a busy signal. Today I got a recording - will call back later. I just wanted to see how you are and tell you I love you.

One final thing –I don't understand your attitude

toward finances. It is out of question that you might not have a phone - that's my major link to you and Rachel - and it doesn't do anyone any good for you all to be so stubborn and prideful. I'm not rich but I'm not a pauper either. Would you help me if the roles were reversed?

The plan now is for Val and I to drive up next Saturday. I'll be talking to you before then, but I hope nothing else happens to prevent this. Val did get the paper, cartridge, and ribbon you needed and we will bring them. I am also talking to Hospice here - no news yet.

Have I completely worn you out? What has happened is that it's Mitchell Luther King Day and we have a holiday. I've been writing all this in between loads of wash and visits to grandmother. Good thing I don't write often. You'd never survive.

Jim, I love you. - have always and will always. I would give anything if it were I and not you.

X X X

Mom

The Mitchell's came as often as possible to see about Jim and his new family. Val and Mike, both devoted siblings, came with quiet resignation, reaching out to him and trying to help him hold the line against his enemy. The Anderson's came to love the Mitchells and enjoyed their visits. Kate tried not to interfere with their time there but often came to help Rachel prepare and relieve the added strain of "company in the house", only because she knew that having the house in order and food prepared was important to her daughter.

Chapter Forty Four

The News

The Mitchell's abnormal life went on in this way until early March of 1992. That was about the time Rachel called Kate into town and told her the news. Something else had been added.

They were pregnant.

You cannot put yourself in someone else's shoes and you can bet that no-one could have been comfortable in Kate's when she heard those words. The only thing she could see during those first moments was the years ahead, the years Rachel would live while raising four sons alone, instead of three, and where was Kate going to find herself in those circumstances?

She realized that Jim looked hurt when she finally recovered her senses. He was waiting for her to say something, anything, but she was speechless. Rachel looked at her mother with a mixture of joy and anxiety. Then things came back to Kate, things Jim had said during the past year and also something 'Rachel had said on a recent trip into LaGrange. She had cried and said she was afraid that someday, she would forget Jim's eyes and the way he smiled at her. She didn't know what she would do without that memory. And more than anything else, Jim wanted to leave something, a mark that would show that he had once lived.

He waited and so Kate said, "Well, this will certainly leave your mark, won't it Jim?"

The discussion led to when, etc. and Kate went home, mulling over the words she would use to give Keith the news.

By this time, Rachel's grandfather (Anderson) had suffered a severe stroke and had difficulty speaking. The family visited with him at the nursing home and when he was told about the coming blessed event, he grinned a silly little grin for a long moment and then muttered, "Well, Jim's sure doing a whole lot better than I am."

Chapter Forty Five

Rotten Eggs

The Andersons' surprise was no less than that of the rest of the extended family and the citizens of Fayetteville. You can be certain that the hows of the whole situation - a paralyzed man fathering a child, were a hot topic in many gatherings

Before I begin this portion of their story, I want to say that many of the people of Fayetteville were kind and wonderful. I also must explain that some people are like rotten eggs which float on water. These individuals began to surface in Fayetteville.

Theirs was a profound lack of understanding. They obviously knew where babies came from but evidently didn't know the facts of the reproduction process very well.

The folks in the small town were not as kind as Great Grandpa had been. They seemed to arrive at the conclusion that Rachel was apparently stepping out on Jim and this pregnancy was proof of that.

Immediately, the boys began coming home angry about the names Mom was being called by those "molded Czechs" I mentioned earlier. Their taunts were cruel and they didn't leave them at school. Late at night, the older boys drove by the house and repeated the names they had been using. On one occasion, a beer bottle was thrown at Rachel as she walked to the small grocery store near their home. It shattered and glass fragments cut her legs.

Jim was furious along with the rest of the family. This was one of those moments when a man feels compelled to protect his family. The wheelchair tightened its grip on him and he knew he could do nothing.

During this terrible time, the women gazed at Rachel with disgust, openly judging her in their ignorance. The men looked at her, revealing their thoughts in a different way. Some demonstrated open admiration, possible envy of her relationship with Jim, while others sneered with contempt.

Kate was a witness to these behaviors. She held her tongue but dreamed more than once of giving some of those busybodies what they deserved.

The final straw came for her shortly after the bottle incident.

Rachel had sent the boys down the street to the Catholic Church to buy a pot of stew during one of their fund raisers. The stew was dished out into the kettles purchasers brought with them. When the boys started to go in the front door of the church carrying a stew pot, some of the boys from the congregation barred their way and told them their mother was a whore and they didn't belong there. These individuals followed this rebuff by ripping off the seat and kicking the lights and reflectors out on the boys' bikes. When Rachel told Kate what happened over the phone, both parents made a quick trip into town.

This provoked another one of Rachel and Keith's disagreements. Both father and daughter had hair trigger tempers and this was a common thing for them. Keith insisted that this time, he was going to talk to those boys fathers and tell them what their kids were up to. He'd had enough. Rachel vehemently protested that this would only make things worse for the kids.

Kate's thought was, "How can things possibly get worse?" She honestly didn't know.

Keith went home and called the boys fathers in spite of

Rachel's wishes. Prompt intervention was promised.

A priest who needed to tend his flock…

Keith wasn't the only one still steaming over it. Kate had to vent her rage too. When Keith was finished talking to the parent, she called the Catholic priest and gave him a very large, steaming piece of her mind. She told him he was having some troubles with his flock and needed to take care of business. When she explained her reason for saying so, his response was that he had no control over what the people were doing. She told him that he was a lousy priest if that was the case and he needed to do his job. A lot of people who supposedly went and sat in that congregation and listened to him had evidently not been taught the lesson about not judging others, polite behavior, God's love for everyone, and what was his job anyway? He asked what she wanted him to do. She said, that was a *dumb* question. If he needed to be told, the behavior of those kids and the words they were using were coming straight from the mouths of their parents, those fine upstanding praying members of that congregation. Maybe they couldn't help their lack of education, but someone needed to do a little educating of the whole bunch. They needed to be told a few things and as Kate saw it that fell into his job description. She ended with a heartfelt statement that a lot of people in Fayetteville were not good enough to walk in her sweet daughter's shadow. They had no idea who she was and they obviously didn't care.

The poor man didn't know what hit him. Kate felt better after venting her anger and never knew if his congregation was chastised or not but things improved after that for one reason or another.

While all of this was going on around her, Rachel had still not seen a doctor about her pregnancy and was not doing well. One of her friends from Houston provided an ultrasound to be sure the baby was healthy. This was not a standard ultrasound. This one was detailed, studying the baby's heart valves, brain, and everything possible to be shown on such a study. A video was taken and for the first time, Jim saw the face of his son. The boy's face was like a photograph. He looked exactly like his dad. Seeing the film brought the truth of what was happening home to Jim. He wanted to watch the video over and over. He said he didn't see the resemblance.

Kate thought he just wanted to hear her say he was wrong.

Chapter Forty Six

Troubled times

Two major events headed for Rachel like a steam roller. Jim was becoming weaker. He needed her more and more, and the baby would soon be born. Rachel seemed to be deteriorating as quickly as Jim. During the last three months of her pregnancy, her blood pressure shot through the ceiling. She finally saw a doctor who started her on blood pressure medication, but it was not helping because exhaustion was the cause and sleep was impossible.

As had happened before, Jim came down with a cold. This was a terrible situation because he could not swallow. Rachel stayed by his side, suctioned his mouth and helped him with the drainage a cold brings. She kept a vaporizer going and washed his face often with warm cloths. He suffered and Rachel suffered as well.

Even when he was well, Jim woke her every five minutes during the night. He was having more difficulty breathing, his bones pressed against the thin flesh on his body, and he had to be moved constantly.

During the day, Rachel took care of Jim and her sons, and waited for the birth of her child. Her legs swelled and she suffered debilitating headaches. Kate spent as much time as possible trying to help but the major burden was on her daughter.

Stress fractures……….

The stress was pressing on their marriage now. Arguments between them came more often.

Rachel used a saying "Where's MY biscuit?" when she was feeling left out of things and during these days there were definitely no biscuits for Rachel.

Sometimes, she couldn't stand to hear one more request for anything from anyone and she would tell all of them to shut up and fend for themselves, including Jim. She would leave the room, return abruptly, do whatever Jim had needed, and leave again without speaking to him or the boys. The day didn't contain enough time for each one of her charges to have a fair share, and her own needs were completely lost in this scrambled pressure cooker.

If Jim scolded one of the boys, he was usually doing it to try to make them help their mother. Meanwhile, Rachel was feeling guilty because she didn't have the time she wanted to spend with her children and she certainly didn't want the cause of it making their life miserable.

The boys invaded her time with Jim and Jim invaded her time with the boys. It was a vicious circle and while she was trudging around it, she was carrying an abundance of last straws on the back of her very pregnant body.

When Jim's family planned to visit, this usually provoked an argument. Probably because he was a man and hadn't been on a woman's side of the fence when company was on its way, he could not understand their visits causing distress for Rachel. It wasn't that she didn't want to see them, or didn't love them. The problem was, she couldn't stand anything, not one more thing to be added to her extremely tiring, complicated life. No matter what Rachel did, the boys always had the house looking like a haystack and she did not want anyone coming for a visit to find her house in a mess. Jim's family always insisted that she not worry about the house or anything, but that was an impossibility for her.

On occasion, Jim threatened to return to Galveston. When he did this, Rachel would say, "Alright go ahead, but I'm not taking you." At one point, he wanted to call his mother. Rachel dialed the phone for him - with gusto. He spoke to Pat for a long while and she convinced him to stay where he was.

All was not coming up roses in those trying days.

Following one such altercation, Jim asked Kate if she thought it had been a mistake for him to marry Rachel. Was he fair in having done so and how could she love him as he was. Kate studied him for a moment, considering what to say. The sadness and uncertainty was clear in his face. She answered, "Jim, I know only one thing for certain. My daughter fell in love with a man, deeply and completely. When I look at you, I still see that man. The one she fell in love with is still here, every bit of him, and I can fully understand why she loves you."

He answered nothing, just raised his eyebrows as he always did in his way of hopeful acceptance.

Chapter Forty Seven

All Rachel wants

Kate surmised that Rachel and Jim were wasting extremely valuable time and she had never been a mother who didn't speak her mind. Their arguments would erupt in her presence as though she was invisible. This probably happened because she was there like Rachel's third arm much of the time. With the combination of their tempers and Kate's mouth, she sometimes ended up refereeing their fights.

She could not bear to see them tearing at one another and when she tried to tell each one they were wrong about the other, they decided she was favoring the others point and view and usually ended up mad at her.

Wherever the break through occurred, it began when Jim finally heard Kate's statement about changing Rachel's mind. She said, "Jim, no-one has ever been able to change Rachel's mind when it comes to disciplining the boys. You are batting your head against a brick wall. That's all I am trying to tell you, a brick wall. I know you are frustrated because you want to be a real dad to the boys, but all she wants you to do is love the boys, talk to them, give them advice and be there for them. That's what she thinks a dad should be. She doesn't want you to change them. In fact, she will never give in to that. I know she won't. You've heard her fight me. Don't you think I know what you're up against? What is happening is - you and she are fighting a losing battle with one another, torturing one another when the kids are not even the real reason you are arguing. The important thing here is not who wins the argument or makes the best point, the main thing is, you and Rachel don't have a lot of time left together. You *do not* have time for this. You are spending extremely precious days banging heads. You have to believe that I see all that the boys get by with. I also see where Rachel is right about a lot of things and you are right about a lot of things, but she has had the sole say about those boys all of their lives.

You two love each other. Why don't you just do that and make the time count. Enjoy being together. This is too important.

Kate helped with everything physically possible after that and shut up about their disagreements. At some point, they worked their way through it.

Jim's needs increased and usually Rachel was the only one who could help him.

Chapter Forty Eight

In the Midst of Life Again

As Rachel's workload increased the family looked for ways to alleviate any part of it and make things easier for everyone. One choice would be to move the furniture around to suite the current situation. As in other things, Jim hated change. Change was symbolic to him. Change meant he was getting closer to the inevitable. He was furious when Rachel moved the computer to a different location. Shortly thereafter, she moved more than the computer.

Jim and Rachel's bedroom was in the back of the big house. Jim slept late in the mornings. Kate believed he did that on purpose to give Rachel a little time with her sons- getting them off to school, and then he waited longer- letting her drink a cup of coffee in the quiet. He could not wait long in any case and then she began frequent trips down the long hall to their room to see what he needed.

During one of Kate's visits, she watched Rachel drag her swollen body out of the chair and trudge down the hall. Kate suggested that they move all of the furniture from the back bedroom into the living room. Jim's bed would be there in the room with the fireplace. It was a huge room, probably 30 X 50. His computer could be beside the bed and a sitting area, a large couch and chairs could be on the other side.

It sounded like a good plan to Rachel.

They moved Jim into the family room and closed the double glass doors between there and the living room. The windows of the door were covered by curtains so Jim would not see what they were doing.....and now to begin. They called for help and soon the entire family was in on the move. Before Jim could argue, everything was ready. The glass in the front door was wallpapered, letting in light that showed its pattern but blocked the view from the outside to give Jim privacy. Candles were lit, the bed was fluffed and it was time to wheel Jim into the room. When he saw what they had done, tears came to his eyes. At first they thought they had made a terrible mistake but when he finally spoke, they discovered that he was overwhelmed that they wanted him, always, there in the front of the house with the family. He would never miss out on anything, no matter how bad he felt or if he stayed in bed all day. Rachel would have easy access to him at all times. It would be easier on both of them. No one said, but Kate guessed that the entire family spent the night in that room that night and many thereafter, gazing into a roaring fire in the fireplace or watching TV together. The boys probably curled up on the couch near the bed or on the couches in the family room a few feet away instead of going to their own rooms. Kate told Rachel, "You all sleep all over the house like a bunch of cats anyway."

The big TV was placed in the corner, blocking a door that opened into Patrick's room. It was visible from anywhere in the room. Rachel rented movies and Jim was back in the midst of life again.

This eased Rachel's troubles a little but not enough.

Hospice????

The only hospice available at this time was the one in Yoakum. In order to have hospice care Jim had to go to a doctor in Galveston for a six months to live diagnosis. He did that and then they discovered that the nearest hospice care was in Yoakum, Texas. They were contacted and for numerous reasons, this service was not what Jim needed. He was on pain medications, had bad headaches and trouble breathing. Oxygen was added to his needs.

Nurses to help.........

Finally, Jim asked his family for help and they hired nurses to come in and bathe him each day. They administered his medications, feeding tube care, bathed him, and other things, then left. Most of the continual care was still up to Rachel but she would not have made it through without those nurses. They took the pressure off and Rachel seemed to gain a little strength to go on. It helped Jim's spirits too.

Chapter Forty Nine

At the hospital

Rachel's blood pressure remained high and she grew more exhausted with each day. When her labor began, Kate was frantic about the blood pressure, but the doctor's unconcerned method of care was to tell the nurses to add more blood pressure pills. He did this until the dosage was extremely high. Kate told the nurses that Rachel was so exhausted from the long months of caring for Jim and her children that she was afraid she would not have the strength to have the baby. Three times during the long night, the nurses began preparations to move Rachel to surgery. They said, "With her pressure as high as it is now, the doctor is going to want to perform a C section and take the baby". Each time they spoke to the doctor on the phone, he instructed them to give her more medication.

Jim had lived a full eighteen months longer than the doctors had predicted when October of 1992 arrived and most of the life insurance money from his policy was gone. Once again, they were stretching to make it through the month.

In this situation, Rachel had no health insurance and the birth was to be paid by Medicaid. Medicaid pays on its own terms and doesn't pay the doctor's full fee. Kate felt that this had an effect on the doctors care since Dr. Mueller stayed at home in his bed and refused to come to see her during that dangerous night.

Whatever his reasons, Kate had an urge to shoot the man on sight.

Rachel labored through the pain filled night and Jim waited at the house with the boys. Kate was with Rachel and could not remember after that night exactly who was taking care of Jim. Perhaps Keith was there. This was the first time she lost track of what was happening to Jim.

Somewhere near the end of her labor, they finally gave Rachel a spinal block but this was done long after she needed it. The block was done incorrectly and numbed only one side. Kate begged Rachel to ask the doctor to please take the baby before both were lost. Rachel didn't want to bother anyone, so the wait continued.

When the baby finally arrived, he was in trouble. The delivery room exploded with nurses and staff and Kate knew something was wrong. She asked one of the nurses what was happening. All she would say was, "The mother is okay."

Kate told her, "I have been begging the nurses to get the doctor up here or to let me talk to him. Since I wasn't the patient, they wouldn't do that. So, if we lose either the baby or my daughter, this hospital and that doctor will not be the same when I finish with them."

Kate's mother's hackles were up. She was so afraid she could hardly breathe. She whispered in her heart "Oh God, please help them. Please take care of them. Only you know how important this is."

An amazing capacity ...

Finally, the kind nurse came out and announced that the baby was out of trouble and everything was alright. Kate immediately loved everyone again and pushed her way into the delivery room to see Rachel. She gave the doctor a look that said, "I'm here and I'm not leaving." Rachel held her hand and cried. This had been the most difficult of all of her sons births, and two of the boys had been born at home with no pain medications or doctor's care.

Kate went back outside and the same nurse who had answered her questions wanted to talk to her. She knew about Jim's illness. They talked for a while and in the conversation the nurse said, "Your daughter has the most amazing capacity for love I have ever seen."

Chapter Fifty

Proud

Kate left the hospital and went directly to see Jim. His mom was at the house with him when she arrived. That new grandmother went out the door as Kate came in, heading for the hospital to see her new grandson. As they passed one another, Kate looked up and saw Jim's worried face. She quickly reassured him and told him Rachel was doing well...and...he could never, ever deny being the father of that little red headed Mitchell at the hospital. "He's the spittin image of you. He has his mother's hair but the face is you."

He grinned and said, "You're imagining that he looks like me. All babies look like themselves. They never really look like anyone.'"

This was one debate Kate knew she was not going to lose. She answered, "You wait until you see him."

Jim told her he was going to the hospital when the nurses arrived with a van. He wasn't waiting for her to come home. Kate was instructed "not to tell her about his surprise." Knowing Rachel, Kate went to the hospital. Her daughter looked awful following the suffering of that long night and didn't feel like combing her hair. She became aggravated at her mother for fussing over her and finally Kate told her, "He's on the way but he doesn't want you to know he's coming." This "lit the fire" under Rachel and she immediately began primping and fussing over the need to wash her hair.

They didn't have time for that.

Within moments, the entourage' arrived at the door. There was a commotion outside and Rachel immediately thought something was wrong with Kevin. Kate went out in the hallway and then rushed back in to reassure her.

The commotion had been the arrival of her husband. Almost immediately, the nurses wheeled Jim into her room.

Within this open door in time, Rachel and Jim's eyes said everything as they looked at one another. She sat beneath the light above her head holding the baby in her arms. Kate leaned forward and placed a pillow in Jim's lap, and positioned his arms and hands where they would be if he could move them himself. Kevin was then centered in that cradle… and their wonderful little boy saw his daddy for the first time. Father and son looked at each other for a long moment.

Kate whispered to Jim, "Speak to him. He knows your voice already. Let him know who you are."

Rachel reached over and gently picked up one of Jim's atrophied hands. She placed it on their baby's soft cheek, caressing it as Jim would have done in other circumstances. Several of those in the room caught their breath at this and tears began to flow. The crowd which was literally stuffed in the doorway (doctors, nurses, orderlies, janitors and other patients) began to disperse quietly. Those who remained were asked to leave. Kate left with them.

Jim wanted to be alone with his wife and son.

Chapter Fifty One

Three weeks

Little things pleased Jim intensely and Rachel knew what to do. There were many little things during those days shared by father, son, mother and brothers.

Rachel always placed Kevin beside his daddy to sleep, near Jim's head so he could feel his son's breathing and hear all of the little gurgles, smacks and grunts. Right away the baby developed the habit of holding onto his dad's mustache in his sleep. Sometimes Rachel put his tiny fist close to Jim's hand so he could grasp his finger.

One day, Kevin was laying on a pillow in Jim's lap as he sat in his wheelchair. Rachel placed Jim's arms on top of the baby to hold him. This could have worked well but babies wiggle and move like water when they feel the need.

Rachel was working in the kitchen and heard Jim desperately calling out to her. When she looked into the room, Jim was nodding with wild eyed fear at the baby, who was now casually folded like a cat over the cord to his light talker. In spite of Jim's efforts, Kevin had slowly slid off of his lap, down his leg, ending up near the floor. Rachel rushed in and saved the day. The baby was calmly drooling and staring intently at Jim's shoe, unaware that there was a problem about his position. "Look, he's tougher than you think. Babies are like little rags. See? He thinks this is another new fun thing."

After that, Jim didn't want to be left alone while holding Kevin. Rachel was never more than twenty feet away in the first incident but that didn't matter. Jim was taking no chances.

The light talker was capable of singing. Jim sometimes sang 'I'm A Little Teapot" to Kevin. Kevin would concentrate on Jim's face during these performances, probably wondering why Daddy's mouth didn't move like Mom's when she talked.

It became apparent to everyone that Jim had willed himself to live until the birth of his son. The only bad thing about the coming of this gift was the change in Jim's acceptance of his approaching death. He told Rachel that he was no longer ready to go.

Letters...........

Jim busied himself at his computer, writing letters. This was extremely tiring for him and he expressed concern that he had not finished his book and had probably waited too long to complete the letters. Writing these words, these goodbyes, was an acceptance, the climbing of one of those final plateaus in his six year journey with ALS.

How many times must a man face such a reality?

Kate told Jim he "must be someone extremely special in God's scheme of things. Only those who have great strength within themselves, those wonderful creations with a destiny we cannot know, are placed in such circumstances as those he was facing." She always felt a sense of blessing when they had those talks, the blessing being that of knowing this brave young man.

Chapter Fifty Two

Jim's new favorite nurse........

The nurses Jim's family had hired to help out were wonderful during these days, giving Rachel the time she needed to care for Kevin. All of the nurses were pleasant and kind. It's not unusual to pick a favorite from any group and Jim had his among his nurses. His pick was a very strong African American lady.

(I have racked my brain but cannot remember her name. If you are reading these words, I apologize to you dear friend. Please forgive this slip on my part. You were so beautiful that I only remember your ways, your gifts, and your wonderful spirit.)

This was the only nurse Jim would allow to physically lift him from his bed or chair and place him in the bathtub. She was also always jolly, laughing at Jim's jokes and sharing things about her life and family. Her personality and sweet spirit were the reasons Jim played a trick on her.

Before she came that morning, Jim worked intently on his light talker…adjusting the sound until he produced a deep voice similar to Dean Martin's. When she arrived, the chatter began with this happy lady whirling about the room. Jim had a slight grin on his face the whole time. At one point, she asked him what he was so full of smiles about. He didn't answer, just kept grinning. She went on about her work, preparing him for his bath, bathing him, and then at the end of his grooming. During her term of caring for him, he had to wear a catheter. This was not internal but was fitted similar to a condom. Kate and Rachel listened from the next room as she began to replace the catheter.

At last there was a beep from the light talker and the deep voice boomed out, "Oh baby, baby!"

The nurse squealed and ran from the room. She told Rachel, "I'm never going to touch that man again. No Sir. I'm never going to touch him again. You're gonna have to do it. Mr. Jim, you oughta be ashamed of yourself."

Jim was laughing.

The nurse then turned on her heel and went back into the room, giving Jim a sound lecture on how a gentleman ought to behave.

She forgave him but remained wary of the light talker.

Chapter Fifty Three

The trip to the farm

In early May, Madelyn's little girl was born, becoming the first Anderson granddaughter. She was a delicate pretty flower whom Kate began to call Happy because of her constant smile. She would become the little mother of the boy cousins and they all doted on her or picked on her most of the time. The family was growing and Jim was there being a part of the celebrating. He was now Daddy Jim as well as Uncle Jim to Andrew and Jackie.

He had made many visits to the farm spending time with the family, but in the last months, Jim left the home in town very little. The family wanted him with them, particularly when Elyse and Andy came out from Austin or when Madelyn came from Houston with little Jackie.

Andy was an outdoor guy who loved to build campfires outside at night. Since Jim was interested and knowledgeable in astronomy it was decided that Jim had to join the family at the campfire, no excuses.

The kids all loved to ride in Grampa's trailer. Jim had always been one of the boys, so about midafternoon, they hooked up the trailer, loaded Jim in his wheelchair and with all of the boys riding in the open trailer, the family headed for the farm. It was a wild ride for Jim, with the wind blowing around him. He was a small boy again, as though his head and arms were being held out beside the window of a car, and he was flying like a bird. When they arrived he looked rather windblown and rumpled but was wearing a broad smile.

Keith and Kate no longer lived in the big yellow house. Their new place was nearer to town and the property joined the paved road. The small farm had 16 acres of land which rolled gradually from the highway down to a dry creek bed with pools of rainwater here and there. A mist often crawled along the creek which was lined with tall pecan and live oak trees. The Anderson's land sloped up the far side beyond the creek, ending at a barb wire fence along the back. Beyond that was an old wooden barn and farm house. A hill climbed higher past this house and over the horizon just out of sight was the farm the family lived in when they first moved to Fayette County. The land open and flat on the east side was a pasture occupied by half-starved cows belonging to a neighbor. On the West - the next farm was a thick stand of oak trees. Before you reached the west fence of the home place, a tin barn stood watch over a fish pond.

The farm was a haven for the family, picturesque and calming to the spirit. This is where they took Jim that day and right away, Andy had the boys scampering, gathering wood. Soon a huge fire was blazing.

The crows squawked among the trees near the creek before dark, adding their voices to the blue jays, mocking birds and the high screech of the killdeers who paraded around on toothpick legs. As night settled in, frogs at the pond sang to the family and now and then a night hawk swooped past inspecting the gathering as they sat out beneath the stars and swapped tales in the cool night air. The back of Jim's wheelchair was lowered and he stared at the sky, telling the boys how to locate the constellations.

It was such an event that those who were there cannot look into the night sky without remembering the family and how they were during those precious hours of that particular evening.

Chapter Fifty Four

Light Beam

On **November 11ᵗʰ, 1992,** Kate made her usual trip into Fayetteville to see about the little family. The stress level was reaching its peak now on Rachel and Jim. When she arrived that morning, Jim was trying desperately to finish his letters. A neck brace might have helped a little but he refused to wear one. He said it hindered his ability to move but with his weakness, he was having trouble hitting the right letter with the light beam on his talker. He was continually asking Rachel to adjust the light which was worn on a strap over his forehead. She became frustrated with the light and Jim became frustrated with her.

This pattern repeated itself over a period of hours during the morning, even though the real problem was not the position of the light.

Included in the trouble that morning was the foot rest Jim relied on to push himself back into his chair without assistance. He insisted that there was something wrong with the footpad because his foot kept slipping off. Rachel and Kate worked for over an hour, trying to arrange the padding which had been increased slowly over the time of his illness. Padding was added to the arms as well as the footrest. Everyone in the family often lifted him back into position in the chair but he wanted to do as much as possible for himself. Giving up this ability was another loss in his war against the disease.

At some point, perspiration was pouring off of Rachel and Kate.

Jim gave up before they did. He began almost apologetically, "it's okay. It's not going to work."

They were exhausted but couldn't stand the look in his eyes so they continued long after he said they could stop trying.

Both battles were lost. It was a bad time for all three of them.

When Kate started to leave that day, Jim thanked her and apologized for all of the trouble. She stood there in front of him with her hair in an extreme mess, face red as a turkey and scoffed at him. She could not recall later, but she was certain that her appearance added to the moment. Whatever it was, it was something dingy that she did or said and Jim started laughing. Everyone ended up laughing. As was so often the case, the laughter was a pressure valve that released the deep sadness of the day.

Kate headed for home and once again, he called out with the light talker, "I love you, and....You're wrong."

Chapter Fifty Five

Jim's discussion....*everyone will forget.*

He often said, "no-one will even remember that I ever lived. All of my friends have already forgotten me. I haven't done anything with my life. I didn't have the time I thought I would have. That's the worst of it, the feeling that I've not made a difference." They tried to reassure him but he was a skeptic and wanted proof of everything. Kate had to be careful that she didn't paint herself into a corner with him. He usually enjoyed this confrontation and it often distracted him, bringing him out of a dark mood.

There was a bitter side to Jim, bitter because he had been deeply hurt by all of those people who had once been his friends. Those people he somehow believed would never leave him, had disappeared along the way. They told themselves it hurt too much to see him suffering and changing before their eyes.

Kate thought, how selfish such an attitude is. What is this thing in the human spirit that we make excuses for ourselves, feigning love for someone and saying we cannot bear to see them suffer? What of their suffering? Are we to leave them in a pain they cannot flee from, simply because we do not care enough to make ourselves suffer with them? To look away is not love. If my brother is cold and the cold will kill him but not me, why do I not stand with him in that cold and comfort him? By our living, we all leave traces in the sand of life. The traces that will remain are those made on the human spirit, our own and the lives we touch along the way.

Chapter Fifty Six

Call the Family

On the morning of the **thirteenth of November**, Rachel realized that Jim's kidneys were no longer functioning. The nursing service was called and told that the time was near. Keith took the boys out to the farm to stay with him and Rachel called Jim's family. His mom had been to see him the day before. She had told him goodbye that day as his condition was evident.

When the boys went out the door, Kate told Aaron that Jim was dieing. He asked "Now?" and his face turned gray when it was confirmed. She asked him not to tell his brothers just yet. Kate thought they probably had at least twenty four hours or so before the end.

The morning began with Jim struggling for breath. He tried lying flat, sitting up, resting at an angle. Nothing helped but with each request, Rachel moved his head, propped him on pillows or whatever he wanted. She was distraught and Kate could hear her spirit screaming. Back and forth, she moved in a pained daze, trying to care for Jim. Kate took care of Kevin.

When the hospice nurse arrived, she instructed Rachel on Jim's medications and talked to him about his condition. She didn't stay with him. No one understood why. Perhaps it was because the instructions from Jim were that he was not to be put on a respirator under any circumstances. He refused a false semblance of life by living that way. His body was shutting down. The time had come. It seemed to Kate that all of Jim's family, and now the nurses were leaving the final struggle in Rachel's hands.

She was diving out of a plane without a parachute and no one, even her mother, was going to be able to catch her as she fell.

Jim had had a hospital bed for over a year but refused to lay in it. He would have no part of it. He had been refusing even on this day when it would make things easier. Finally, the nurse convinced him that he should use the bed so that Rachel could move him more quickly and with greater ease. The clincher was when she said it would help Rachel. And so, for the first time, Jim was placed in the hospital bed.

He had reached the final plateau.

After the nurse left, Kate sat with Jim for a while as they waited for his family. They looked at each other, the long discussions between them now past. What could she say to him other than do as she always had? She spoke her mind. What she was thinking at the moment was how this reminded her of those times when she sat with each of her daughters during their hours of labor, waiting for each of six grandchildren to be born.

Somehow sitting there beside her now son, the process of birth and death felt the same - moving from and toward the presence of God.

She told Jim her thoughts. He nodded in agreement with the comparison. She wanted to tell him not to be afraid, but she wasn't him and knew she had no right to say such a thing. She asked if he had ever decided anything about Jesus and he said he had. They talked a while longer.

She said, "I love you Jim. You mustn't worry about Rachel and the boys and I'll try to do something with your work on your book and your poem about the dream." She made other promises and Jim nodded to let her know he had heard her.

He said, "I hope somehow you can have the same kind of relationship with Kevin that you have with Sean." She answered, "You have nothing to worry about there. I will be here for him and all of them, as long as life allows."

At an earlier time, she had told him, "If I could, I would reach inside that body and snatch you out of there." He had answered. "I wish you could."

The rest of the day became a blur for all. Everyone moved about doing necessary things and carrying a tremendous stone in their chests. At some point in time, a breathless Val came through the door and rushed to her brother's side. Jim's brother Mike arrived about the same time.

The first look on their faces asked, "Are we in time?" This was a day they had tried to prepare for since they had been told of his diagnosis years before. Now, it was here and their hearts were breaking. The one thing they knew they could do was to be there for him as they had promised. They were here, and he was aware.

Courage cannot be purchased, is not served up in bottles, but there was a huge supply of it there in the Mitchell house on Bell Street that day.

Around midnight, perhaps much later, Rachel discovered that the nursing service had not left enough pain medicine for Jim. She called the service and they in turn ordered the medication from the pharmacy in LaGrange. The service contacted Rachel, "The medication is ready and waiting for you." Val and Mike volunteered to go with Kate or in her place. She insisted they remain there with Jim. That's where they belonged, beside their brother. He needed them.

Kate raced into town, arriving at the pharmacy concurrently with the very sleepy pharmacist. She apologized for having to disturb him and he said his heart went out to the family and wished he could do more.

She did not know how long she was gone but as soon as she arrived, Rachel gave Jim an injection. He had refused the oxygen and Rachel was trying to get him to keep it. The oxygen was not prolonging things and he did not have to suffer without it. He refused.

Later, how much no one knew, Kate went into the kitchen and began to make a fresh pot of coffee. Everyone needed something, perhaps the smell of the coffee brewing would help. While she was in the midst of this task, Rachel cried out, called his name, and someone said, "It's over."

It so happened that the Anderson family often said a silly little blessing at dinner. ..."God is great. God is good. Let us thank him for our fuhd." The boys pronounced the last word oddly to rhyme with the way Texans say the word good. At the moment Kate heard the cry from the living room, she was trying to remember the twenty third psalm, long set to memory. Somehow, she could not remember it and began saying the little God is great verse.

She believed that when death comes, the soul moves through the family on its way and listens to the thoughts of their loved ones. She smiled at herself there alone in the kitchen. Jim must have gotten a laugh out of that dumb little verse I was saying and said to himself..."you really are just as goofy as I always thought you were."

She hoped in her heart that he also felt the love this family had for him.

She called out to his spirit when she returned to the room and said, "Jim, I hope you find that all the words I spoke to you of God are true." They stood there by the bed, his brother Mike, his sister Val, and Kate. Rachel knelt down, her head resting against his face...and a mother listened to her daughter's pain. The letting go was almost more than Kate could stand to hear. The sound of Rachel reaching out to him across that chasm they all looked into that night became a wound in her own heart that would not heal.

Jim need not have worried about his courage. He died bravely, only waking often from the morphine induced sleep, asking how much longer. He called for Rachel constantly. She remained beside him and he accepted comfort only from her. Mike and Val were there as they had promised, assuring him that they were there, telling him of their love for him. He expressed his gratitude and love for the family and looked at Rachel with remembered moments evident in his eyes, whispering again and again, I love you.

Chapter Fifty Seven

A brother's final gift.....

They didn't call legal authorities immediately. Rachel, Val, Mike, and Kate sat beside his bed and said little. They wanted to keep him there with them for a little while longer. Rachel was battling the pain and Mike muttered something about not knowing what he was going to do without his big brother. Mike and Kate went to the kitchen later and she asked "Do you want to help Rachel bathe and dress Jim before the officials come?" His first answer was a definite no. She told him to give it some thought. "It would be a loving thing to do and perhaps help you when you are remembering. This would be one last gesture of love for your brother." Shortly after that, Mike and Rachel were working together with this gift to Jim.

Somewhere toward morning, Rachel was becoming confused from stress and exhaustion. They tried to talk her into sleeping awhile. She said it was impossible. Somewhere in the discussion, Kate remembered seeing George Burns in an interview after his wife Gracie died. He had said he could not rest until he finally crawled into Gracie's bed, and discovered that he could sleep there. Kate told Rachel about this and said "Why don't you go in there and lie down on Jim's side of the bed, hold his pillow next to you and see if you can rest."

She agreed and soon fell asleep with Jim's pillow cradled in her arms.

Three Dads: Patrick, Sean, and Aaron (holding Kevin)

Chapter Fifty Eight

The service

Mike and Val took care of the arrangements for the funeral service. It would be simple as Jim had requested and was to be held at the only funeral home in Fayetteville.

That afternoon, the family walked together the *short* three blocks to the memorial service. Kate walked with the three small knights and they talked a little about the future. One of the boys said, "Kevin won't ever know his dad, he won't ever have a dad." Kate answered, "Oh yes, he will. He has three." She continued. "He has you boys. You will all have to take care of your baby brother and teach him things boys should know. Can you do that?" They said they could and seemed to square their shoulders as they accepted that thought.

The sun was shining on that cool November morning. It was another blessing.

The family was surprised when Aaron read aloud a short note he and his brothers had composed to Jim. It was scribbled on a well crumpled scrap of paper and said "this is something my brothers and I wanted to say to Jim. We didn't have you long enough but you were a great dad. Mom and all of us are going to miss you, Daddy Jim, but we know you've gone to a better place. We love you."

A letter Jim had written to the family and his poem about the dream were read aloud by Mike and Val. His favorite CD, *Somewhere In Time* provided the only music.

After the service, they gathered in the family room and tried to comfort one another. Rachel sat in the floor holding Kevin. Andrew pushed his new baby cousin Jackie around in a clothes basket and the older boys sat nearby. The extended family stayed for a short while, gradually saying their goodbyes.

Jim's mother left Fayetteville that afternoon. She and Kate embraced and Pat said something about Rachel and her gratitude for all she had done for Jim. Kate said, "My daughter and your son have taught me many things. I need to thank you for sharing him with us. For me, the pain of losing him is far more than I had planned to allow when he came into our lives."

That was the moment, that rush of pain and understanding mentioned earlier in these pages. Truth and God's purpose fell upon Kate's spirit as she said those words. She suddenly realized that she had not known her own child before her love for Jim revealed who she was. Her narrow minded vision of what she thought was right for Rachel had been placed beneath a brilliant light. From his wheelchair, this young man had shown her how foolish she was to think any of us know everything about one another or have control of our lives, and that a man's strength is not in his physical body. It comes from his soul.

Chapter Fifty Nine

Their Letters from Daddy Jim

After his funeral, Rachel would no longer answer the phone and so Kate told her to let the phone ring twice. If it stopped and started again it would be her. Rachel would not go to the door. The boys did that for her. She was inconsolable and the boys remained beside her, each suffering in his own way. The letter Jim wrote to them was printed, one copy for each. The older boys went to their rooms to read theirs alone and Kate read one aloud to Patrick. Later, Kate found one tear smudged letter. She never knew which boy it belonged to.

They talked about their letters among themselves and then went to Kate, huddling around her in the family room a few days after Jim's death. Aaron, the designated spokesman asked, "Grandma, do you think Jim loved us like he said in his letter? I mean, really loved us?"

She answered with a hug for each one and said, "Yes, I believe he truly loved you. He loved you very much."

They considered what she had said for a moment before Sean spoke up in his raspy voice. "Well, at least we had a real dad for a little while, didn't we? "Yes, you most certainly did," she whispered

Mother and daughter went together when the mortuary called saying Jim's ashes were there. The label on the small box said November 16, 1992, which happened to be Rachel's thirty fifth birthday. She read the date and began to cry. She said, "Two days ago, Jim asked me what I wanted for my birthday. I told him, only you."

Rachel's sister Elyse painted the vital statistics inside the lid of a small urn and gave it to the family to be used as a temporary container for the ashes. Rachel placed it on the mantel until she could decide what to do. Having it there seemed to comfort the boys, who sometimes patted the side of the jar and talked to Jim. The whole family got into the same habit after a while.

The urn remained there on display in the center of the family's life.

Chapter Sixty

Poignant moment....

The most poignant moment occurred a few days after the funeral when Rachel found an odd collection of Jim's things. His mustache brush, his signature stamp, and other such personal items had been placed in a small mound on Jim's hospital bed beside a small piece of cardboard. Some words were scribbled on the cardboard in a child's hand. It looked like Sean's.

Rachel left it there undisturbed for a very long time.

She had said in the beginning, "Mother, he says all the things a woman needs to hear. It makes no difference to me how he looks, if it will only be for a little while, or what people have to say about it. I love him. I love his spirit and all that he is or ever was. I'm going to marry him and we are going to be together.

Please understand."

Chapter Sixty One

Regrets

Kate had regrets about Jim, the main one being that she did not hug him when she wanted to. Somehow, she was always afraid of invading his space. That fine young man who was so helpless there in a wheelchair and finally in a hospital bed. He might have needed that hug she was afraid to give. He had no way of letting her know that and so that was added to other things that went unsaid and undone.

Another thing she would change if time were rolled back to the night Jim died would be the absence of the boys from that moment. The adults thought they were protecting them. In truth, they were uncertain when death would come.

In hindsight, she realized she had been foolish to not consider the boys need to be with him.

When the boys were told that Jim had died, they were furious, furious that they were not allowed to be beside him to say they loved him one more time and tell him goodbye. They forgot that those were the exact words they had said to him when they left the house that previous morning. They had had time to think of that moment during the months that Jim was with them and surely had special things they intended to say. An apology would never be enough to make this mistake up to them.

Keeping them away was always Jim's request. He expressed his fear of not dieing well. He did not want the boys to remember him as a coward or make them suffer by seeing his fear. He had faced his death over and over in his mind but he could not be certain how he would hold up when the end came.

……..Keith, Rachel, Patrick…

Rachel was never the same after she lost Jim, though she tried. Life was a climb up a mountain road. You may wonder why the word was is used here. It is used because at this writing Rachel is no longer living. Depressed and lost, her health spiraled down. In the days shortly after Jim's death, she began sleeping for days on end or the reverse, could not sleep for long periods. She shut herself off from the world with the exception of working at night. No longer a nurse, burned out, she worked at Target or home care of the disabled, anything to support her boys. She moved like a ghost through each day, each year. Her spirit clung to her sons who were all that mattered other than her parents and sisters. She lived almost fourteen years after Jim's death. Through those years she often asked Kate and her sisters to take care of her boys should anything happen to her. The answer was always yes, but you aren't going anywhere.

In spite of her own unhappiness, Rachel the constant caregiver, visited with her mom every day and they talked on the phone throughout the day. A sweet voiced inquired in earnest about the health of her dad and Kate, "do you need anything? Are you depressed or okay?" She helped with her father's illness as he was constantly in and out of hospitals after his transplanted kidney failed, and worked on projects for the church with Kate. She referred to Kate as "sweet mama" and showered her with gifts, large and small. A cache of special candy and cookies was kept on hand for her mother and she watched for headaches she could cure by brushing her hair or easing any problem her parents or others might have.

The empty chairs….

Keith, Rachel, two grandmothers, and Patrick

They were separated from the family beginning in January of 2006 with Keith's death, Rachel in June of that same year, and Patrick in October of 2007.

Keith Anderson was a quiet man who suffered much more than should have been his share during the last thirty years of his life. He was a man of tremendous courage, though he never knew it. Handsome in his youth, a loving gentle husband for 45 years, sweet in his spirit, he wanted nothing more than the happiness of his family and to be remembered by his grandchildren as a loving grandfather. He succeeded.

Then came Rachel, who filled the family and Kate's life with treasured moments, the first born, was taken suddenly at the age of 48, a friend, forever there for everyone, editing Kate's novel and encouraging her always. The only thing she ever did to harm her mother was to leave her alone in this life without her. Near the end of her life, Rachel had roses blooming in her yard, a garden outback and Moonflowers thriving along the fence outside her living room window. Her boys were in touch and coming around often with Sean and Kevin living at home with their mom. She seemed happier than she had in years. The family knew her health was poor but were unaware of how delicate she really was. She suffered from asthma and the beginnings of emphysema. Whether asthma or emphysema were the cause, her lungs shut down suddenly ....and Rachel was gone.

Jim had asked the boys to hug her every day for him.

They would if they could.

Kate prayed that God would send another soul mate for Rachel. A heart as kind and capable of love as hers deserved much more than two and a half years of happiness, but that was not to be.

Jim's mother Pat died shortly after Rachel and in the same month, Kate's mother also passed. Their deaths added to a period of grieving that left the family in a state of stunned disbelief. The bad news seemed endless.

Then in October of the following year, a freak accident at work took Rachel's son Patrick, who was only 21 years old. In transferring merchandise from a day's sale back to the warehouse, he was thrown from the back of a van and died of a massive head injury. His organs were donated to the organ program and many lives were saved. Six foot four plus, he was a handsome young man and a beautiful child who treasured his mother, tortured his brothers and cousin Jackie, helped support his family, and made them all laugh till they begged him to stop. His was a life unfinished, full of promise with all of the best of it before him, but we have no power over such things.

They all were blessed with giving, loving spirits and they were Andersons for a little while.

When the family was taken to their knees with the loss of these sweet spirits, they looked backward and saw the life of Jim Mitchell. In those moments they drew from all that he had taught them. He had prepared them for those dark days, strengthening their resolve to continue and value all of life that remained. No matter what, they were still the family. The circle had been broken but their love was intact and would remain.

When the family speaks of Jim and Rachel and that time he called Light Years, the talk always includes laughter and remembering the goofiness, the cherished fun the family had, and of course the tears are always there beneath it. The two of them gave all of those months of intense living. It was part of the life lesson the family was to learn.

Even in their suffering, their lives provided an awareness of the beauty and joy of simply being. Jim told Rachel often that he would not have known her if he had not become ill. Therefore, if he had the choice of being well and never knowing her or being as he was, sharing his last days with her, he would choose this end to his life. He was adamant about this fact and would not accept anyone doubting the truth of it.

Chapter Sixty Two

Miracles in Our Lives

The night before Rachel's death, the family angel must have touched Kate and told her something was coming. As they embraced before she left for the evening she whispered in her daughter's ear. "You are so dear to me, you have always been so very dear to me." Rachel looked at Kate and answered. "Same here, Mama. Same here." They held one another for a long time and Kate felt a strange tug at her heart. The next day, Rachel died suddenly. The coroner did not allow Kate to hold her in her arms before they took her away, and so this became their final goodbye.

Though you may not believe it, Rachel came to Kate a few days after her death. She stood behind her mother's right shoulder and it was as if Rachel leaned forward and spoke clearly in her soft voice, "I am here sweet Mama. I'm here." She repeated this three times and in the seven years since that day, Kate has not heard her voice again though she is certain Rachel is there as she has been since the day she was born - beside her.

Most of us have many miracles in our lives and we don't always share them with one another.

We should.

OO

Epilogue

Letters

Mostly excerpts....letters from Jim..............

∞

November 12, 1992

Dear Aaron, Sean and Patrick,

Since you are reading this letter, I know you have been through a hard time. I'm sorry things turned out the way they did, but we didn't have much choice about the outcome did we? I have to tell you all that you are great and I wish I could have stayed with you and watched you grow into men, just like I wanted with Kevin.

Your mother has a very difficult job ahead of her, raising four sons, and so I am counting on all of you to take care of her and one another. She is a very special lady. She does not judge people and sees their heart instead of the way they look. She will need all of her boys to help her in the years ahead. She will be lonely and most of the time she will be tired from work and worry. I want you to hug her for me every day and treasure her.

I have to tell you that before I came to live with you and your mother, I wondered how you would treat me. You surprised me by accepting me as your dad and sharing your mother with me. I took a lot of her time away from you and yet you didn't hate me for it. We had some bad times, that's true, but that's unimportant. Remember only the happy times, and we had plenty of those. I tried to tell you as often as I could that I love you. Believe it. It's true, even now.

I wrote some things in my letters to Kevin, telling him not to lie and other things he should and shouldn't do. I would like for each of you, my first three sons, to read those letters to Kevin and understand that I am saying the same words to you.

Thank you for every moment you gave me, for moving my hands for me, moving my chair, feeding me, and helping me like you did. Look out for one another.

Don't let other boys run over you or hurt one of your brothers, and be good boys.

Don't worry about me.

See you later,

Love,

Daddy Jim

Excerpts from Jim's letters to Kevin:

The first letter was written August 14th, 1992 (prior to his son's birth) and was very short. Most were that way as Jim tired easily and these things were difficult for him to write. He was unable to finish the letters he wanted to write.

Dear Kevin,

I would like to talk to you in person but that is not possible. You will be getting these little letters from me at different times during your life. You will have received all of them by the time you are in your early 20's, that's the plan. I will have written them myself even though when we found out about you I was wheelchair bound, and couldn't really move very well. Ask your mother about how I became your dad. I am going to have to rely a lot on your mother to explain certain things about me.

. . . . .

Dear Kevin,

When your mother told me I was going to be a father, I was very happy. It took a few days to really sink in and when it did, I realized that having a child of my own was more important to me than I ever thought it would be. I was so lucky to have been able to be a dad to your brothers and I love them but having a son that is part of you is a special thing. . . . .

I only wish that I could have been the kind of dad that you deserve and the kind of father I wanted to be. God has other plans for me although at this writing I can't think of anything else that would be more important than being with you, your brothers, and your mom, but God knows what he is doing, I think.

Dear Kevin. . . . . . .

. . . . It will be tough growing up without a dad around but you will not be alone. Your mother is a great woman. . . . . . .and you will have your big brothers. Alright

son, this is important for you to learn. When your mother talks to you, it's very important that you really listen to what she's saying. Being a good listener is something I want you to be.......A man who listens first,, and talks later, is a wise man...so be a good listener.

Remember, Aaron, Sean, and Patrick haven't had a dad around either. They saw him once a month on a weekend maybe, but that's still not the same.

....

Dear Kevin,

I want you to always remember that with love anything is possible. Your mom, Aaron, Sean and Patrick took on a lot when I moved to Fayetteville, but they made my life so much more than it was and they made me very happy. I think that marrying your mother helped prolong my life.

(He explains about his life before his illness and that even though he loved sports it is not important that Kevin do the same as he did but.....) "Whatever you decide to do, give it all you've got.

Dear Kevin,

You may have wondered about the symbol at the top of all of my letters. It is a symbol for a light year and it was my adopted special sign. Your mother had one made for me that I wear on a gold chain. If she hasn't given it to you yet, ask her for it. It's yours. You can wear it if you like or you can just keep it somewhere. I ask you to one day give it to your son, and make a family heirloom of it. I'd like that......

It's hard for me, knowing that I will not see you grow up, but that's the way it is. As I write these letters to you, I'm thinking about what I can say that will make a difference in your life, but I have no way of knowing what the future will bring. All I can tell you are the very basic things of life.

The most important thing to me is honesty. Always tell the truth, don't lie. Next, never break your word. If you say you're going to do something, make sure you do it. Your family comes before all else. Don't put anything in front of your family. Be compassionate to your fellow man, but be careful. Make sure your fellow man is who you think he is. When you're doing something, work hard at doing it right. Work smart. Always stand up for what you believe in and listen to both sides of things before you make a decision on which way to go. And finally, know when to be quiet and when to speak. That was something I never quite learned how to do.....and one more thing. Never be afraid to ask for help when you're having trouble with something.

For now, I'm saying goodbye. Always remember that I love you and I will be looking out for you.

I love you,

Dad

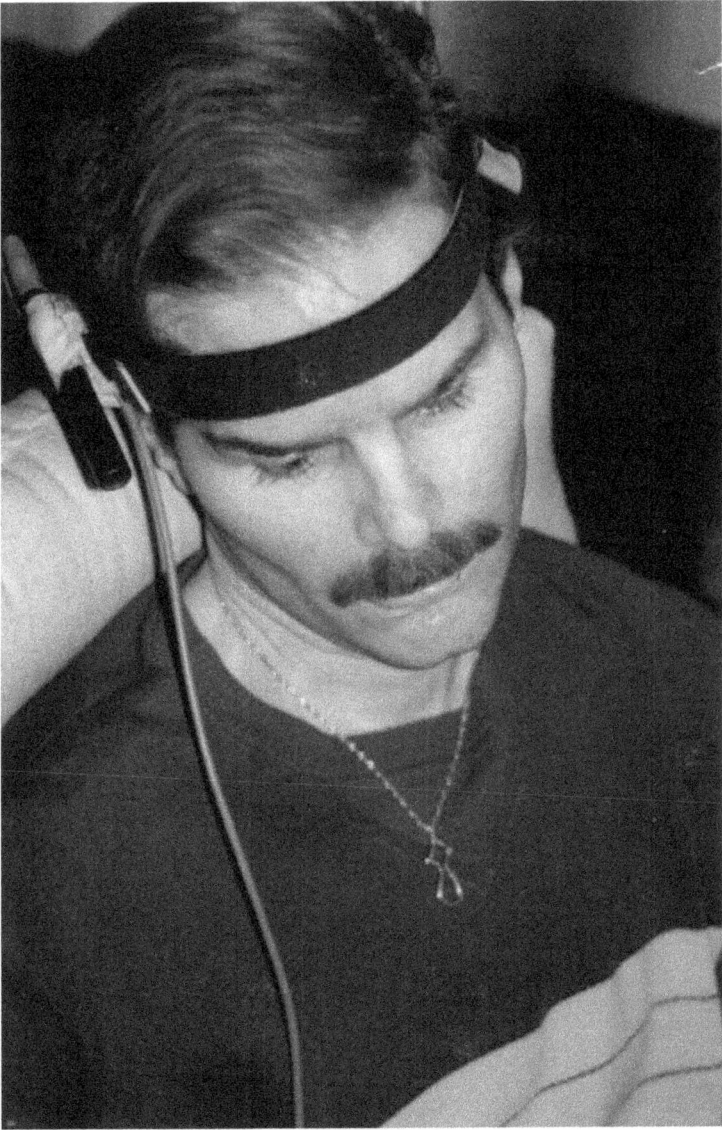

Daddy Jim

Jim wrote many poems. Some were personal to Rachel. The following poem was read aloud by his sister at his memorial service.

The Elusive Dream–

One of Jim's poems

I had that dream again last night, the one I always have.
I dreamed that I was free again, running across the land.

I wonder where it comes from this dream I always have,
Perhaps it's part of the maze of my mind, bound only by limitless time.

Can I go to this place where dreams are lost and found,
Or am I trapped forever in the place that I am bound?

And will I find answers to the questions in my mind
Or will I be like so many men and never have the time?

Why does it repeat itself, bringing me up and then back down
Teasing me into happiness like a two faced clown?

When all is said and life is done and I dream that final dream,
I hope to find that place in my mind where life really is a dream.

I had that dream again last night, the one I always have.
I dreamed that I was free again, running across the land.

Rachel

Rachel's thoughts…copied from her writings.

Both sides of the looking glass

I worked for over 10 years as a nurse, the last 6 of those years dealing almost exclusively with long term or terminal illness and permanent disabilities.

By falling in love with and marrying one of my former patients, I have been given the unique opportunity to stand and glance through both sides of the looking glass, and I have been surprised at the extent that it changes your perspective.

Mother's book is a collection of the experiences, the needs of one family. As difficult as it has been for us, we have thus far been spared many of the most traumatic aspects of this. While my husband's illness is terminal, and the anticipation of what lies ahead of us makes each day a trial to be endured; his physical suffering is minimal, he is not in pain that cannot be diminished. His suffering is that of frustration, anger and a sense of loss. Whatever the degree, it remains painful, debilitating, overwhelming.

I realize now that as a nurse I was guilty of behavior I have come to find so abrasive from often well-meaning people, comparing this situation to others on an "it could be worse" basis. In our eyes, facing death in your mid-thirties is a worst-case scenario. I have also realized how unjust I was in judging how well a patient or family member was handling the strain and hurt. If I were to grade my track record up to this point, my overall score would be exceedingly low, a great deal lower than some of those individuals I considered lacking when I stood on the outside looking in.

A message to others who are caregivers....

A nurse's advice from the other side of the looking glass

A. *Don't compare an individual or family's level of pain, or their reaction to it to anyone else, ever.*

B. *Advise friends and family of the patient:*
Don't draw away from them...
Let them know that you understand that your relationship, even they themselves may change because of what they are battling, and that you can and will maintain your friendship or contact with them through these changes.

C. *Truth: People facing a death of a loved one are hurt by statements such as I can't stand to come to see you because it upsets me so to see (patient or the family) this way...remember they are to deal with the situation without respite. It is better to say, this is very difficult for me, please be patient with me because I want to be with you.*

D. *Keep in touch. These situations are very isolating, not only because friends draw away, but also because the care of the person who is ill requires so much work. Moving them may be too difficult. A phone call, and especially a letter are wonderful expressions of love. It helps the patient and family to know that they are not forgotten.*

E.   *Let them talk it out. This may be the most difficult aspect of helping. I have been told during all of those years of home health nursing that one reason the patients and families became so dependent on their nurses was that the nurses allowed them to talk about their anger, and grief, and death, - subjects that make most people very uncomfortable.*

Don't feel that you have to come up with words of comfort or answers...any questions they may ask, such as why is this happening to us doesn't have an answer. They need someone willing to listen and understand.

Watch what you do. It is easy to slip away, shifting gears in the middle of an important conversation. It will spoil a necessary healing moment. You must be prepared for endless repetition, perhaps even disjointed senseless rambling at times, when you open a floodgate, you can't always control the water's flow, and incoherent dialogue does not necessarily signify a breakdown.

In my experience, there always came a point in the discussion when they would say, "I know you care about my child, but you cannot possibly know how much this hurts me. Of course that was true, the anguish you must feel in losing a child or in watching the hell that their lives can become during a long term illness can be compared with no other.

For our own family, we did not have nurses at our disposal most of those long months. Fortunately, we did have a very close knit family who would listen, and I will never be able to express to them how much it helped us.

Rachel

A letter to Rachel from Kate…..

My Rachel,

We shared a great deal in your short life as mother and child, but I always thought of you as an old soul, probably much older than I. This was never clearer to me than in those days that involved your Jim. You taught me so much and now those things that once perplexed me have become memories most dear…these days are past my darling daughter. Although I feared for you when it all began, you and Jim taught me many things. You were one of those rare people capable of unconditional love and both of you exhibited amazing courage. My pride in you and my love for you both is immeasurable.

Mama

Closing thoughts....

So many people, didn't understand Rachel's ADD difficulties. They saw her disorganized struggling, the boys school problems, nights in a home that never slept, and her absence from family gatherings as a lack of effort. In her own years of living with ADD, Kate had sometimes had the same misunderstanding.

There is an excellent book called "Driven to Distraction" It is a good primer for anyone trying to understand this particular functioning problem.

Kate had tried to change Rachel all of her life, tried to bend her, shape her, as parents will, so she would be like everyone else. She was trying to help but was making her child's difficult life, more so.

If this story will in any possible way, cause a reader to look at their own offspring with eyes of understanding, no matter what the basis of their difference is, this little book may have helped a little in the scheme of things.

We are all different, and strangers, even to those closest to us. It is significant that we give one another the opportunity to be ourselves. To make things better, it is imperative that we accept and love that individual who does not fit the mold society projects as perfect.

Since those days, **those light years of existence** and Rachel's giving and extraordinary love and devotion, Kate has remained in awe of her daughter, this brilliant girl who was tagged "scatterbrained" and suffered too long because of the ignorance of others. She did not deserve the strain in her life produced by society's presumed claim upon her individuality.

The same is true of Rachel's sons. The freedom she gave her boys was appalling to outsiders. She was judged and scorned because of her methods of parenting. Time and the life her sons lead will prove her right or wrong.

Aaron and Sean are married and have become fine men. Aaron is the father of two children. Sean is still waiting for that blessing in his life. Kevin is working on his college degree, still uncertain of his end goals but working at making something of his life. He works to support himself while in school.

Rachel and Jim would be very proud of all of them.

Special recognition:

Following Jim's death, his younger brother Mike, an attorney who served in the Texas State Legislature, worked to pass legislation that would prevent the type of move the insurance company took against Jim. Now, thanks to Mike, the citizens of the state of Texas are protected in such a way that their coverage remains the same when transferred from another state. **Thank you, Mike.**

About the Author

Barbara McAllister also writes under the pseudonym of Rebecca Grayson. She has published one novel which is now for sale on Amazon.com. It is listed as Rebecca Grayson's LIAR (a true crime case from 1926 Texas). She is also a published poet and songwriter and is in the process of preparing her children's books for publication. Look for LITTLE TOCK and THE CHILDREN ARE AWAKE coming soon on Amazon.com. Ms. McAllister is married and lives in League City, Texas. Her husband Mac is currently illustrating her children's stories and provided this book cover. ONLY THE LAUGHTER is a love story about her daughter (whom she calls Rachel in these pages) and Rachel's husband Jim who was her patient and suffered from Lou Gehrig's disease. Within this book you will laugh and cry with the Andersons, witness the beauty and struggles of life and understand the lessons they learned regarding the true value of time.